ALSO BY MARLENE EVANS

Pattern for Living

Pattern for Living Teacher's Manual

Cancer: My Enemy, My Friend

There's Life After Cancer

Help Lord! They Call Me Mom

Comfort for Hurting Hearts

*Christian Womanhood Cookbook
and Homemaker's Guide*

I'm Going to Live Until I Die

New Hope: Be the Parent You Were Meant to Be

Redbirds and Rubies and Rainbows

A Daily Chat with Marlene Evans Around the Bible

Marriage Without Divorce

Relationships Without Regrets

MARLENE EVANS

Kids Without Chaos

THE LIFE SERIES

Copyright© 2001
Christian Womanhood
8400 Burr Street
Crown Point, Indiana 46307
(219) 365-3202

Second Printing, 2002

ISBN: 0-9719019-2-9

All Scriptures used in this volume are taken
from the King James Bible.

COVER DESIGN:
BerylMartin

Printed and Bound in the United States of America

Dedication

Susie Taylor

Susan was born December 20, 1951, in Little Rock, Arkansas. On her forty-seven birthday, she looked at me and said, "Mama, I wonder what all those doctors who said I wouldn't live to be five years old would think if they could see me now?"

There was a slight pause; then we both roared with laughter as I said, "Susie, all those doctors are either dead or in some nursing home, suffering the trials and tribulations of old age!"

That's the way it has always been with Susie and me. It's not that we enjoy the suffering of others, but we always find and focus on the lighter side of most every situation.

Susan had some brain damage at birth—a cleft palate and Mongolism. That's what it was called back then. Now the term used is Down syndrome. We were told she would not live beyond the age of five, and it would be so much better for her and our family if we "put Susie in an institution where they know how to take care of her special needs."

My belief then was and still is that absolutely nothing happens to us in this life which has not been permitted or allowed by God. He did not cause Susie's afflictions, but He did allow this to happen for a reason. I took Susie home and treated her as if she could learn everything any other child could, but at the same time, not expecting her to do so. Because of this philosophy, I was never disappointed and then when she did learn, we would have one great big party. We laughed and clapped our hands and rejoiced in the goodness of God, thanking Him for Romans 8:28–39. God has given me a great and wonderful gift, and I have tried to share this gift with the world.

–Susie's Mom, Maretta Taylor
Corinth, Mississippi

To Susie with Love

Sometimes people infer that I am really good to Susie as if she's a "project" to me. That always "ruffles my feathers" a bit, and I have to calm myself by saying, "That just shows those poor people don't know the joy of a Susie Taylor in their lives."

Susie is a friend of 25+ years whom I met when her brother attended Hyles-Anderson College where I teach.

When Susie, her mother, and her brother lived near the college, Susie began volunteering for me as my work involved the ladies' dormitories and *Christian Womanhood.* I was happy to know that she received her first paycheck from *Christian Womanhood*—and she earned every penny of it!

Susie sat in the lobby waiting for workers from my office to give her errand assignments. She is the only person I can remember—including myself—who could **always** be found when we needed her. If she were given no errands in a morning or 25 errands, she did not leave her post. If she wanted to go to the snack shop for a drink or the restroom, she always checked out and then back in with my office. You can't put a price tag on that kind of dependability.

Susie and I have gone out to eat, spent time in my home, and taken some trips together. I have never known whether or not she ever got her feelings hurt. She is so easy to be with because she apparently has no expectations and is happy for everything she gets.

Susie does have preferences and opinions, but the most difficulty I have in our relationship is getting her to express those preferences and opinions. She constantly defers to others.

Susie has read completely through the Bible 28 times, and it shows! One time I took her to Teibel's dining room for lunch, deciding I was going to stay there until I could "stump" her. I would give the name of a Bible character or story and let her tell me about it. I was the one "stumped" first!

Susie says she is retarded. If she is, I could wish more of us fit into that category!

Susie Taylor is the reason this book is being published at this time.

–Marlene Evans

Acknowledgments

"A word fitly spoken is like apples of gold in pictures of silver." Proverbs 25:11 has always been one of my favorite verses. This book of many words joined together to form sentences and paragraphs and chapters has been the work of a team—a stellar team of friends.

My heartfelt thanks to Leslie Beaman, Connie Eyer, Gina Eyer, Rena Fish, Jane Grafton, Cathy Kimmel, and Linda Stubblefield. Each labors in a unique way to complete me in the writing and publication of my books. Each contributes valuable insight, and each brings her excellence to my work.

My heart goes out to those of you who have upheld me in your prayers and have nurtured me with your cards, letters, phone calls, and gifts of love. All of your words have been fitly spoken words. You have been an inspiration to me, and your continued support and commitment to me have caused me to dream greater dreams. How I thank each and every one of you.

It is my desire, as well as the wish of my helpers, that the words contained within the pages of this book will be like "apples of gold in pictures of silver" in your life.

Contents

Foreword

Not a day goes by I don't give thanks that Marlene Evans is my mother. I am truly blessed by her love and wisdom. Her love, care, attention, lessons, talks, insight, and *hours* of listening mean everything!

My husband and children share my feelings. They make statements such as, "I will always remember how I enjoyed being with her in the Smoky Mountains." "I loved the time Grandma and I sat on the dock and talked for an hour...and the way the sparkles went across the water."

Mom loves with all her strength, all her being, and all her heart. It almost seems that she performs magic to move mountains when necessary to help meet needs in the lives of those she loves. We love her for all the things she does with us and for us, but most of all, for the love with which she does them. I love her, oh, so much!

–Joy Evans Ryder

$\mathscr{I}$t Isn't Easy Being a Kid!

Jesse Evans

———

"His children shall seek to please the poor, and his hands shall restore their goods." (Job 20:10)

Excite children to look for opportunities to help those who do not have what they have.

It wasn't easy being a kid—not during the thirties and forties anyway. No, sir! No matter how good a childhood I had, it was very difficult to figure out adults. I was always listening and watching to catch any clue I could, and I was still left groping in the dark.

For instance, take the matter of insurance. My dad got insurance against Mom being sick, and she got sick anyway. Grandpa Zugmier was insured against an accident, but he fell in the flour mill where he worked and had to have his leg amputated anyway. Grandpa Fauver was insured against death, and he died in spite of the insurance policy.

Dad could write on pieces of paper, go into a building with bars in front of a man, give the paper to the man, and get money from that man. Then, Dad would tell me he didn't have enough money to get us ice cream cones. When I suggested writing on a piece of paper, he'd laugh and say, "Money doesn't grow on trees."

Questions = Solitary Confinement!

Adults always said, "Just ask a question when you don't understand." I would ask and they would say, "Find something to do, 'Question Box.' I'm tired. Don't ask me one more question."

One time Mom and Dad took me to an Evangelical United Brethren Church Conference at a campsite in Milford, Nebraska, where they had a banner over the front of the auditorium and sawdust as a floor. Because of being allergic to sawdust at four and five years of age, I'd hack and then say, "Mom, what does that sign say?" Then a few minutes later, I'd ask, "Dad, what does that sign say?" Each time they'd tell me the banner read, "Follow Thou Me."

Somehow I kept forgetting it. I guess my coughing distracted me. Finally, Mom marched me out to the ladies' restroom—all because I asked a question, I guess. After all, I didn't need to go to the restroom.

Teachers were infamous for nice words like, "If you need help, raise your hand, and I'll answer your questions." I'd raise my hand whenever I needed help, and they'd say, "Marlene, just stay in your seat and figure it out yourself." I was isolated and put in solitary confinement.

World War II Was in Vanilla!

The war was really puzzling to me as a child. Part of the war was fought in "Vanilla." Mom had bottles of vanilla in the kitchen cabinet, but I really couldn't see a war being fought in them! Yet, the newsmen on the radio kept talking about problems in "Vanilla" in the Philippines.

That brings up another problem. At the very same time that there was trouble in "Vanilla" in the Philippines, I was learning the books of the Bible. Mrs. Viola Krauss, my Sunday school teacher in the Blue Springs, Nebraska, Evangelical United Brethren Church showed me the Philippines right after Ephesians. Can you beat that?

Sick in September

My mom often told me to keep my ears open and pay attention so I could learn without asking so many questions.

In trying to follow that advice, I stumbled onto a real brain teaser.

When visiting my great-grandma in Thayer, Kansas, I overheard Mom and my great-grandmother talking about an aunt who had gained a lot of weight in the stomach. My great-grandmother looked at me, winked at my mom, and told her that this aunt was going to be sick in September. Now, we were in the middle of the summertime, and my curiosity was truly aroused. I'd always been told if you planned on being sick on Sunday or on a test day, you weren't really sick. Yet, here were these perfectly sane, reliable adults aiding and abetting in planning an aunt's sickness months in advance. Can you believe it?

People Laughed at Me!

Sometimes when I asked questions, people laughed at me. They didn't let me in on the joke either. Parents, grandparents, teachers, and other adults who take time to explain could really help kids a lot.

It's rough being a kid, and don't you ever forget it!

$\mathscr{A}$re You Afraid Your Child Is Going Sour?

David Cowling

"And these words, which I command thee this day, shall be in thine heart: And thou shalt teach them diligently unto thy children, and shalt talk of them when thou sittest in thine house, and when thou walkest by the way, and when thou liest down, and when thou risest up." (Deuteronomy 6:6-7)

If you teach your children God's words when you sit, stand, lie down, and rise up, there will be very little time you aren't teaching them one way or another.

Among the members of the medical community, the term "sour" seems to be a popular word for patients whose physical condition is deteriorating. Good doctors, good nurses, and all support people go into a plan of action to try to turn that condition around if at all possible. Poor medical professionals stand around wringing their hands, trying to determine where blame should be placed and arguing over the course of action.

I wonder if parents cannot be classified into the same categories as can the medical people? Instead of wasting our precious time taking our child's deteriorating behavior so personally, why don't we put our "mother's heart" on hold? We could call a "Code Blue" with the air of one who is standing outside the situation looking somewhat detached as she is assessing the job before determining the tools, people, and treatment needed.

Some Possibilities
for Treatment of a Child Going Sour

1. **Be as diplomatic with that young person as you would be with your best adult friend who looks as if she might be headed for trouble.** When I was about 11 years old, my family went on a vacation to Colorado. Since I had been picking vegetables in a truck garden before I left, I sent a card from Colorado to an older man, "Boo" Boughen,

who was the garden owner and boss. Upon my return, my Uncle Charlie (Boo's son) told me I was diplomatic because I sent that card. I had no earthly idea what the word "diplomatic" meant, but I thought Uncle Charlie's eyes and voice sounded and looked as if it were something good.

When I went home and consulted my dictionary, I was really happy. I wish I could say that I have always been a diplomat in working with children—my own kids, my school kids, or my Sunday school or bus route kids.

According to Webster's New Collegiate Dictionary, *diplomacy* is *an artful management in securing advantages without arousing hostility.*

The words in that definition are quite a mouth full on the subject of rearing children. If every advantage we're trying to secure is truly for our child's eventual good for a lifetime, more power to us in learning artful management.

You wouldn't want to dump the whole truckload of displeasure about your friend's poor behavior all at once, would you? Surely we can restrain ourselves with our children and those whom we are mothering.

Instead of "coming off" in such a way that makes it seem we are attacking the child, why don't we ask some well-thought questions to see what is at the root of the problem? "Now you tell me what's wrong with you," and "You just aren't the same girl you used to be," are commands and statement-type attacks which can no doubt be counted on to bring out hostility or cool withdrawal from the kid already going sour. Instead, *"...be ye therefore wise as serpents, and harmless as doves."* (Matthew 10:16b)

2.   **Think more of his or her feelings than you do of your own.** Your child is no doubt already feeling like

"slime" as the kids say. Remember that you can be the refuge, the sanctuary, the oasis, the calm in the midst of the storms of life. If the child sees that you are all upset, he surely will think his feelings of worthlessness are being confirmed. He's thinking, "I guess I really am that bad off if Mom is that far gone because of me."

Instead of looking at the behavior, what about really looking at the child? Later you will have to deal with the wrong behavior, but can't the kid come first—just once? Do you ever wonder what's wrong with him to cause him to perform so poorly? I have so often told my psychology classes at Hyles-Anderson College, "Behavior is always caused, and causes are always multiple." You say, "But I'm no psychiatrist." Praise the Lord! That child in trouble just needs a caring, loving parent at this point.

Do you suppose putting his interests above your own would cause him to at least consider your love?

3. **Get the child alone as often as possible and be ready to give undivided attention.** In Matthew 23:37, Jesus said, *"O Jerusalem, Jerusalem, thou that killest the prophets, and stonest them which are sent unto thee, how often would I have gathered thy children together, even as a hen gathereth her chickens under her wings, and ye would not!"* Has your child stoned anyone you sent unto them or killed a prophet? If the people Jesus was talking to would have run into His arms, He would have gathered them together under His wings. If your child will go with you physically, at least, place him under your wings by:

• Making a game plan to discover every decent interest he has and develop mutual interests as much as you can. (Maybe you'll be a listener or a spectator.)

• Spend time with the child in the woods, out camping overnight, riding in a car, going out for a bite to eat together, or other places where there are few distractions.

4. **If the young person begins talking, listen only! Show or say nothing at this time.** We may need to go to a dentist to have our mouths wired shut preceding this time together, but it would sure be worth it if we could listen once to the child. One of the biggest complaints of children is, "Mom will never listen!" As mothers, we either tune our children out and say "Yes" to "May I go play in the traffic?" or we jump in to talk before they finish what they are saying. *"He that answereth a matter before he heareth it, it is folly and shame unto him."* (Proverbs 18:13) As soon as our children tell us something they think, we say, "You shouldn't think that." Well, maybe they shouldn't be thinking that particular thought, but the reality is they are thinking that thought. If we would stop and listen, we might have some chance to help put their thinking into perspective again. We might be able to make plans to subtly and wisely launch a quiet plan to fight the wrong thinking in spontaneous over-the-table talks or in family devotions.

If you get visibly shocked about your child's thinking, you will get one result. The child will decide she can never trust Mom with her thoughts again. The child will find someone who will listen, at least for awhile. Wouldn't it be best for you to be that one? More than likely if a child or teen feels he cannot tell Mom something he is thinking or feeling, he will turn to his peers, who are not qualified to help him through the difficulty or crisis in a wise and proper way. If a child will not talk at first, enjoy the silence that might prove golden.

The quietest, most sulky young person will have a chance to spill out his feelings as you are listening attentively even to silence, if need be. He has time to muse. *"My heart was hot within me, while I was musing the fire burned: then spake I with my tongue."* (Psalms 39:3)

5.   **Talk about the child's problem with God and only one other person—one who is as confidential as a human being can be. Hopefully, if you are the child's mother, this other person will be your husband, but that cannot always be so.** Many young people will not share their feelings, ideas, problems, or hurts with the people they should be the closest to because their supposed confidant has discussed them and their problems with others. *We are never free, under any circumstances, to make a child's problems fodder for gossip.* Somehow we think a young person is "fair game" for showing off our superior amount of knowledge. Their problems are just as hurtful to them as ours are to us, and we don't want ours to be the "after lecture discussion" at the next women's meeting. It distresses me so to have parents just casually throw out the latest episode in their troubled child's life.

The teaching profession is also infamous for "discussing" the problems of young people. Teachers say they're getting help in their handling of the child, but I don't believe that for a minute. If help is what they need, they don't have to use names—just situations. You say, "But, Marlene, they know anyway." Fine, but they don't have to know it from you. Even the smallest child does not want to be a laughing stock or the object of a pity party. Neither do you nor I. Don't wound the kid's spirit. *"...but a wounded spirit who can bear?"* (Proverbs 18:14b) There's just no use in telling all we know. If someone asks an inappropriate direct question ("Why did Susie get expelled from school?"), answer with "Pray for Susie. All the kids these days need so much prayer." It's never appropriate to discuss another's problems except with God and one person who can help. Most people don't ask about someone's hurt in order to help them, I'm afraid.

6. **Stay in the Word of God and in concentrated prayer for this child for a period of time until the Lord lifts the burden for a while.** You may have some tendencies toward the feelings listed below. Let the Scriptures placed beside the temptation be a start toward getting into the Word of God about the child going sour. Let these and other verses pull you into the Bible. Claim a verse or verses in regard to God's promises for this child. The following are some examples.

- **Worry:** *"Be careful for nothing..."* (Philippians 4:6)
- **Anxiety:** *"...my God shall supply all your need..."* (Philippians 4:19)
- **Despair:** *"...greater is he that is in you, than he that is in the world."* (I John 4:4)
- **Fear:** *"I will not fear."* (Psalms 56:4)
- **Complaining:** *"Giving thanks always..."* (Ephesians 5:20)
- **Vengeance:** *"...vengeance is mine; I will repay, saith the Lord."* (Romans 12:19)
- **Depression:** *"...be of good cheer; I have overcome the world."* (John 16:33)

- **Doubt:** *"In all thy ways acknowledge him and he shall direct thy paths."* (Proverbs 3:6)
- **Disappointment:** *"And we know that all things work together for good to them that love God, to them who are the called according to his purpose."* (Romans 8:28)

"Pray without ceasing" (I Thessalonians 5:17) is the way to bombard Heaven for the kid about whom you are concerned. As you go about your activities of the day, whisper the name of your child over and over to God. Be sure to talk it all out with God on purpose; and then, feeling relief given by God, you can put your mind on others for a while.

7.   **Plan special outings you know the young person will like—ones which will take time more than money.** Perhaps your child would enjoy your getting out pictures of him from the past, scrapbooks, a baby book about which you can laugh together, and anything similar which would cause you to focus on the child and to remind him of good times. Perhaps you can gather all the scattered pictures of the years to mount in a big frame or to put in a book. Some of these things give you and the child common ground on which to meet in order to relate to each other.

Find a way to enjoy any project or activity the young person does and make it your mutual interest too, whether or not you've been drawn to that activity or thing in the past. I doubt many women like mud pies, but they like their little children; and so, in turn, they like the mud pies brought to them. You don't have to like the interest. But do gather around the interest because of the one who is interested. *"We then that are strong ought to bear the infirmities of the weak, and not to please ourselves. Let every one of us please his neighbour for his good to edification."* (Romans 15:1-2)

8. **Write notes to the child every time you see something good.** How about looking for the following in that child going sour? Often the child who is "going sour" thinks there is no hope, and everyone around him seems to reinforce that fact. Be different from everyone else. See some "gold" others don't see and "gold" that even the child himself doesn't see.

When you write to a young person, give a specific example of how you have observed one or more of the following attributes in her life. You could give the word, definition, maybe the Scripture verse (maybe not), and when you saw something nice happen.

• **Encouragement**—helping a friend to see a difficult situation from God's point of view. *"For as the heavens are higher than the earth, so are my ways higher than your ways, and my thoughts than your thoughts."* (Isaiah 55:9)

• **Patience**—accepting a difficult situation from God without giving Him a deadline to remove it. *"And not only so, but we glory in tribulations also: knowing that tribulation worketh patience; And patience, experience; and experience, hope."* (Romans 5:3-4)

• **Joyfulness**—maintaining a spirit of cheerfulness despite physical or any limitations *"And he said unto me, My grace is sufficient for thee: for my strength is made perfect in weakness. Most gladly therefore will I rather glory in my infirmities, that the power of Christ may rest upon me. Therefore I take pleasure in infirmities, in reproaches, in* *necessities, in persecutions, in distresses for Christ's sake: for when I am weak, then am I strong."* (II Corinthians 12:9-10)

• **Endurance**—inward strength to withstand stress in order to accomplish God's best. *"And let us not be weary in well doing: for in due season we shall reap, if we faint not."* (Galatians 6:9)

• **Flexibility**—not setting affections on ideas or plans which could be changed by God or others. *"Set your affection on things above, not on things on the earth."* (Colossians 3:2)

• **Virtue**—moral excellence that radiates from one's life as he obeys God's Word. *"And beside this, giving all diligence, add to your faith virtue; and to virtue knowledge."* (II Peter 1:5)

• **Justice**—personal responsibility to God's unchanging laws. *"He hath shewed thee, O man, what is good; and what doth the LORD require of thee, but to do justly, and to love mercy, and to walk humbly with thy God?"* (Micah 6:8)

• **Orderliness**—preparing one's self and his surroundings so that the greatest efficiency will be achieved. *"Let all things be done decently and in order."* (I Corinthians 14:40)

• **Initiative**—recognizing what needs to be done before being asked to do it and then doing it. *"Be not overcome of evil, but overcome evil with good."* (Romans 12:21)

• **Alertness**—being aware of what is taking place around one so that he can have the right responses to those events and situations. *"Watch ye and pray, lest ye enter into temptation. The spirit truly is ready, but the flesh is weak."* (Mark 14:38)

- **Gratefulness**—making known to God and others the ways in which they have benefitted one's life. *"For who maketh thee to differ from another? And what hast thou that thou didst not receive? now if thou didst receive it, why dost thou glory, as if thou hadst not received it?"* (I Corinthians 4:7)
- **Enthusiasm**—expressing with one's spirit the joy of the Lord. *"Rejoice evermore."* (I Thessalonians 5:16) *"...for the joy of the Lord is your strength."* (Nehemiah 8:10c)

I want to share with you a sample of some notes I have sent to girls at Hyles-Anderson College. The girls who received these notes were not "going sour," but this type of note could be written to a young person who has been in trouble or is in the wings waiting for trouble.

The first note, of course, is written to someone who had sent a note to me.

> *"Probably you do not realize how much it helps me to have you stay in touch with me. Words are the tools of almost all my work now—speaking, teaching, writing, and counseling. I love words and their influence for good. You sent me words, and I appreciate them."*

The second is one in which I'm trying to show my concern over an infirmary stay.

> *"Sitting here trying to recall my college days in the infirmary, I see a girl in her older teens and early twenties wanting care, love, attention, soup, aspirin, and a heating pad. Some call this nurturing—at least one phase of it.*

"Since there is so little nurturing in comparison to the amount of admonishing going on all over the country today, I want to let you know I care that you are not feeling well, and will leave admonishing up to others for this time.

"You are being brought before the Lord as I leave you in His care. He will wrap you in His everlasting arms and give you contentment and peace if you will bask in His (and my) love."

Each person in our lives is a gift that needs to be handled with care. There are so many emotionally fragile young people. Why don't we handle them with more care than we would handle a fine piece of crystal? After all, a piece of crystal doesn't have an eternal soul.

9. **Waste as little time as possible assigning blame.** Assess the present circumstances and look back only to go forward in a better way. Generally speaking, we spend so much time trying to assign blame to society, television, the youth sponsor, the mother, the father, siblings, preachers, the school principal, and whatever or whoever else we can think of that we are rendered paralyzed to do anything about the present problems. *"Brethren, I count not myself to have apprehended: but this one thing I do, forgetting those things which are behind, and reaching forth unto those things which are before, I press toward the mark for the prize of the high calling of God in Christ Jesus."* (Philippians 3:13-14) If we are reaching back, we can't stretch as far forward. The Devil wants to stop us from doing what we can today. Don't let him have the victory.

10. **Simplify your life however you have to in order to have time to "go for the gold" in your child.** In this day

when houses are not designed for kids, hospitals are not staffed to give comfort, lawns are not for families, schools are not for students, churches are not for sinners, towels are not for dirty hands, and soap is often for decoration rather than use, let's get back to the basics of living.

We have jobs that demand our all in order to gain promotions so that we can give the kids their wants. Provide their needs and give them *you*, and you'll find they won't have so many wants.

Cut to the bone your expectations of yourself—those expectations that have nothing to do with eternal values. Influencing a child for good will live forever—that's eternal.

A mother of mothers, Mrs. John R. Rice, lived with eternity's values in view. At her funeral service on November 13, 1989, some beautiful words were said about her.

> *"Some people live, die, and are never missed.*
> *Some people live, die, and are missed forever. Why?*
> *Because they lived while they lived.*
> *Mrs. Rice lived while she lived.*
> *Influence never dies.*
> *We cannot bury her deep enough to kill her influence.*
> *She will live in and through us for years to come."*

Mrs. Rice was with us during the *Christian Womanhood* Spectacular at First Baptist Church, Hammond, Indiana, just 12 days before she went to Heaven. She was, at that time, giving encouraging words to hurting people and caring more to make time to go for the gold in people than to have her own needs met.

Let's help those young people who have started to "go sour" and all the others, too. Let's start throwing open doors and turning on lights as a way of life.

*Marlene Evans with a class of friends
at Hammond Baptist Grade School*

*The Mike Borsh
family*

*The Ernie Salazar
family*

$\mathcal{L}$ove Is...
Disciplining Your Child

Kaylin Sapp

Brinley Sapp

———

"Thou shalt beat him with the rod, and shalt deliver his soul from hell." (Proverbs 23:14)

Biblical discipline given early in a child's life very well might keep the child from frustrating his parents to the point that the parent loses control and abuses the child.

———

"Withhold not correction from the child: for if thou beatest him with the rod, he shall not die." (Proverbs 23:13)

This type of discipline is not referring to abuse and certainly not to anything that leads to death.

Let us reason together to see what might be one of the greatest ways we could ever demonstrate love to a child and perhaps to a nation.

The topic: *spanking*! Since Proverbs 13:24a says, *"He that spareth his rod hateth his son,"* we can safely assume that he who does not spare the rod loves his son.

Lack of spanking may be one of the top causes for society's major problems. "Time out" in a room alone is the world's current alternative to God's command of spanking a child for disobedience.

In response to "time out," some children sit in their corners loving every minute of being alone and, therefore, not receiving punishment at all. Still other children spend every minute in the corner seething as they plan ways of "getting back" while they grow bitter at being left alone with no one to help put them into perspective.

"Time out" is a method to be used to help a child "cool off" when he is angry or to give him time to think about what he has done. It is not a biblical alternative to spanking.

Withdrawing privileges, if you really remember to follow through, can be a very effective method for teaching that "crime doesn't pay." There are children who "shiver in their boots," and sincerely mean it, when they know they're going to have to have "a talk" with Mom and/or Dad.

Be creative and use all the ways that are successful in dealing with your child but remember that God says a great deal in the Bible about the rod of correction being needed as a method for punishment.

I know that most parents are scared to death to follow God's Word on this, and I understand why. The world is teaching against spanking to the point that the people on talk shows are even bragging about the fact that supposedly 60 percent of the people in the United States now agree that it is wrong to spank. I've heard parents of young children say they are scared to spank even in their own home, especially if it is an apartment complex where the administering of the spanking could be heard and reported. I know of parents who take their young children into the bathroom, put on a fan to muffle the noise, and run the water because they are so frightened about those who might turn them in to the authorities for what they would call child abuse.

I have even heard parents of very young children use a different name for spanking so that the little children will not innocently and unknowingly answer "yes" when someone asks if they receive spankings. Just a few years ago, I can remember how the general public would look with scorn at parents who let their young children get away with misbehavior. The saying was, "I'd give them a good spanking."

Of course, that was because they didn't want to have to be around "bratty" children who made them nervous. The real issue is that when a child does not learn that he will be punished for misbehavior, he may torture society and himself for the rest of his life. One of the best ways we can love children is to help them know that they will have to pay for wrongdoing. Spare the rod and spoil the child is just the beginning of what God has to say concerning the rod.

Also keep in mind the following verses:

• *"Foolishness is bound in the heart of a child; but the rod of correction shall drive it far from him."* (Proverbs 22:15)

• *"Withhold not correction from the child: for if thou beatest him with the rod, he shall not die. Thou shalt beat him with the rod, and shalt deliver his soul from hell."* (Proverbs 23:13-14)

• *"The rod and reproof give wisdom: but a child left to himself bringeth his mother to shame."* (Proverbs 29:15)

Webster's dictionary gives one meaning of a *rod* as *a straight, slender stick growing on or cut from a tree.*

While the world system is calling spankings a leading reason for violence, I am afraid no or too few spankings at a young age is one of the leading causes for violence in our society.

Recently I heard a mother say to a small child, "You do what I told you to do, or I will spank you."

The child responded before a group of others with, "She will not." The little girl had not been talking many months, but she was old enough to know that she would not have to pay for disobedience.

If I remember correctly, Mrs. John R. Rice used to say that if the spanking part of discipline was cared for the first few years of a child's life, there wouldn't be much need of anything similar as the child became older.

When a child is small, we're now saying, "They're too young to understand, and a spanking will hurt them too badly. I just can't do it."

Instead we are waiting until children are beyond our

ability to control with a sensible spanking on the bottom and are beginning to slap, hit at, and bang them around in our frustration. Thus, I reason, not spanking sensibly and early leads to abuse.

I fully realize there have been many abusive beatings in the name of spanking by some caretakers (teachers, babysitters, parents, and other relatives) in the past. But, instead of going on a campaign to teach what a real and loving spanking should be, the world went on a "no-spanking" campaign. We threw out the baby with the bath water.

As the world is trying to be so careful that children are not hurt by a proper spanking, it is leaving those children to grow up to be much more severely hurt by the world. As my good friend Bertha Frye once said, "You teach your child or life will teach him, and life is so much harder than a loving parent."

The child will not like the discipline (possibly best to use the word discipline rather than spanking, although we know that discipline involves so much more than spanking). However *"...no chastening for the present seemeth to be joyous, but grievous: nevertheless afterward it yieldeth the peaceable fruit of righteousness unto them which are exercised thereby."* (Hebrews 12:11)

How are young people to learn self control if they have never experienced control?

In 1989, I still felt safe enough to write Chapter 8 which is "Positive, Courageous Child Discipline" in the book, *Help Lord! They Call Me Mom.* I'd like for you to read some excerpts from that chapter. You can see that I was beginning to realize that you would no longer be applauded for making your child behave, but I still felt that you could follow God's teaching in a discreet way without having someone (perhaps even good friends) report you to the authorities. Let's consider a couple of situations when you have problems with your children. Has your child ever "acted up" in public? Perhaps you have watched someone else's children misbehave. Maybe you've even thought, "Why don't they keep those brats at home?"

Disciplining in Restaurants

What is your response when you are in a restaurant with a child who begins to throw food and have a temper tantrum? If you say, "Okay, let's hurry and get through with our meals so we can take this child out of here," the child knows he is in charge. Therefore, he knows he can be in charge again.

What you **should** do is leave the table with your child (even if your meal gets cold) and take him to a private place to discipline him. Maybe he's kicking and squalling, having a fit all the way. Maybe people are looking at you and thinking (or saying!!!), "Look at that nasty big person who's going to beat up on that defenseless little child." Of course, all of this is embarrassing to you. But it is vital that you take the time to discipline.

Take time to go through the whole situation. Ask, "Why did we leave the table?" He should tell you why. Then say to him, "We're here because you were not behaving properly in the restaurant. When we go to a restaurant, we sit quietly. You were not doing that, so I'm going to have to spank you." Don't even let yourself think about your meal that's getting cold; let it get cold. It can be reheated (even if you have to take it home), or you can have a cold meal. Either of these is better than having a child you can't take out in public because you're worried about his behavior.

Hopefully, that one trip out of the restaurant will take care of the situation, but sometimes a child seems to need to find out if you really mean he has to *always* behave in a restaurant. If he misbehaves again, take him out of the restaurant again, and discipline him again.

Disciplining on Trips by Car or Plane

How many times have your children made your plane or car trips miserable? You've just been in the car two minutes, and they're begging to stop for a snack. You refuse, and they immediately begin begging in that whining tone of voice. The first time you give in just to "get them to hush," you've had it! Now if they stop asking and you want to stop and get a treat, that's fine, because you are in control. Every child needs someone to control him, so you be in control.

When the whining starts, ask your husband to stop the car and have a major overhaul—and it's not on the car either. This will take time. It quite possibly will make you late getting to Grandma's house, but don't worry about that; Grandma will have much nicer children to visit with even if it's for a shorter time. She'll be much more pleased to have them if they are well behaved.

Perhaps the problem has nothing to do with whining for treats. Perhaps the children are fighting with each other about "property rights" in the back seat. If you're a parent of more than one child and you have taken a car trip with those children, you know what I mean! "Mom, she's touching my book."

"But Mom, his book is on my half of the seat."

Again, stopping the car to deal with the problem takes time, but it is time well spent. We must take time to discipline again and again and again.

When your kids see that their behavior is so important that you are willing to do whatever it takes to correct that behavior even if it means being late, they will get the idea that it is pretty important. (Of course, we are assuming that you are in the habit of being on time.) I think our children get the idea that we really don't care that much about how they behave, and I think that they translate that to, "It really doesn't matter how I behave because I'm not that important."

Now don't stop the car when you're angry. Don't stop until you have yourself under control, or the children will just think, "Mom's having a bad day." They won't learn that it's their behavior that is causing the trouble. When you know that you can talk slowly and quietly and that you are in control, then stop. Of course, the younger your children are when you start this, the less time you have to take with them.

Plane trips can become horror stories because of children, too. I've been on those wide-bodied planes and seen one child tear up a whole plane. Flight attendants try everything they know to quiet the child. Strangers will even try because it is obvious that the mother has no idea what to do. No one can sleep or do anything else because of the child. The mother's solution is to let the child crawl up and down the aisle where the flight attendants are trying to serve meals and beverages! Now I know that there's not a lot of space in those tiny airplane restrooms, but they are big enough for some positive, courageous discipline when it's necessary.

Be careful when you discipline. Be sure to spank on the bottom, and make sure it's not child abuse. If you are angry enough that you think you might not be in full control of yourself, cool off before you spank. Be sure you spank in privacy. (This is important for your child's dignity as well as for your legal protection.) In today's warped society there is always the possibility that parents who discipline properly will be accused of child abuse. Therefore, we should make every effort to avoid spanking our children in the presence (either able to see or hear what we are doing) of someone who might report us for child abuse. But, we should discipline our children even though we are concerned about this possibility. How many of you have left the home of a friend or relative because the children were "driving you up a wall"?

You don't have to cut a visit short because of your children. Find out what the problem is. Sometimes children are misbehaving simply because they are off schedule, hungry, or tired. If they are sleepy, have them take a nap. If they need to be fed, your friend or relative will probably give you a snack to tide them over until you get home. Now if we drag our children around shopping until they are ready to drop from exhaustion (without any consideration for their needs), then it's our fault they're being bad. Correct the matter immediately. But if their needs are being met, it's time for positive, courageous discipline. Simply ask to borrow a bedroom and do whatever is needed to correct their behavior. Then you can go back and finish your visit.

Remember, we must be *"wise as serpents and harmless as doves"* as we follow God's Word instead of following a phase through which the world is going. It will be too late when the world finds it's gone wrong and says "uh-oh" as it has so many times in the past.

Do You Think That Too Little Spanking Is Causing Abuse?

A few years ago, I read that Oprah was happily reporting that 60 percent of parents now believe in the "no-spanking" policy for rearing children.

Somehow she nor very few others of the world's counselors seem to put no or little spanking together with more abuse. They really seem to believe that abuse will stop as spanking stops. I believe Oprah and other celebrities have seen brutal whippings and beatings they call spankings. Perhaps they are overreacting to poor parenting and poor teaching they experienced or observed.

I once taught in a school in which teachers walked the halls and stood in classrooms with bo-bo paddles at the ready. I was told that this was the only discipline these kids understood. Those teachers hit on knuckles, shoulders, heads, and whatever else was handy. They never seemed to try praise, fun, talk, or any other way of getting the attention of their classes. I, in no way, call this spanking. I call that type of correction "abuse."

Even a few people who do not believe the Bible is the Word of God can logic out that little spanking equals more abuse. Parents who sheepishly look at others around them to laugh and shrug when their toddler says, "No," may no longer be able to physically haul off the child when he says, "No," at eight or ten years of age. In frustration at not being able to control the behavior of the child, nonviolent parents may become very violent.

Dogs are getting much better training than most children are receiving today. Obedience schools talk "praise," but they also talk physical correction. If a dog isn't trained, it often ruins the life of its owner if it is kept. Many untrained dogs are put to sleep or left at an animal humane center because "he was just too hard to handle. People didn't want to be around him."

Do we care more for dogs than children? No, untrained children are also being given away because, "He's too hard to handle."

If you are saying, "I want to properly spank my child, but I'm scared he will be taken away from me," again I say to read, study, and reread the chapter, "Positive, Courageous Child Discipline" in my book, *Help Lord! They Call Me Mom.* I believe we must learn to properly spank in order to avoid more abuse if for no other reason.

Love your children by lovingly disciplining them! It could well be the best gift you ever give to them.

Marlene Evans with Stephanie Allen

Brittany, Sarah, Nathanael, and Timothy Hawkins

Johnny, Joshua, and James Barnes

$\mathcal{D}$o You Provoke or Nurture?

Kimberly Brock

David Brock

"And he said, Lay not thine hand upon the lad, neither do thou anything unto him: for now I know that thou fearest God, seeing thou hast not withheld thy son, thine only son from me." (Genesis 22:12)

We can trust God with our children. He wants the best for them and loves them more than we are capable of loving them. _____

"And be ye kind one to another, tenderhearted..." (Ephesians 4:32a)

Plan kind words and deeds for others with your children.

Do you ever have the feeling, "Things are out of control! I'm going to kill these little monsters if someone doesn't help me!"

I can tell you exactly what to do with those kids—send them out in the traffic! No, not really. But every mother at one time or another feels she is at the end of her rope regarding her children. And all too often, the end result is yelling, screaming, jerking, and other unkind treatment of the children. I am writing this chapter because I believe that mothers reading this book want to be kind to their children and have a desire to nurture their children. I believe that teachers and other children's workers want to treat the children with whom they work with kindness and respect.

Actually, I believe that every adult should be a "children's worker." Everyone has children with whom they come in contact, and those children need every adult on their side. With all of the divorce, hurts, and confusion in today's homes, there aren't enough "parents" to go around. Of course, I am referring also to people who are parenting those who are not their birth children. Oh, how desperately children today need to be nurtured. There is plenty of provoking, yelling, screaming, and rejection. What is needed is biblical nurturing.

Colossians 3:21 says, *"Fathers, provoke not your children to anger, lest they be discouraged."* Ephesians 6:4 says, *"And, ye fathers, provoke not your children to wrath: but bring them up in the nurture and admonition of the*

Lord." I believe that the majority of the young people in America today are discouraged and full of anger and wrath. Young people are withdrawn, rebellious, and angry because they have been provoked. I am not excusing a young person's wrong attitude or wrong actions. But I do believe that we adults hold the key to helping our young people by nurturing.

Maybe you are asking, "How does one nurture children?" Or maybe you are asking, "What does it mean to nurture?"

The dictionary definition of nurture is, *"training; education; further the development of…"* While so often the word *nurture* conjures up images in one's mind of cuddling or hugging a child, it actually means to teach the children in your care.

Mothers get frustrated and yell at their children for not doing what they are supposed to do when those mothers have never really *taught* their children the particular trait about which they are yelling. I am not saying the mother hasn't *told* the child how to do something; I am saying the mother has not *taught* the child. Telling and teaching are different. We can talk and tell until we are blue in the face without results. ***Teaching is a transfer of knowledge that changes behavior.*** Teaching comes by patiently explaining, showing, allowing the child to try; explaining again, showing again, allowing the child to try again; explaining once again, showing once again, allowing the child to try once again, and repeating this process until the child has learned and knows the joy of victory.

You say, "Mrs. Evans, that takes time!" Yes, it does, and then you have to do all this over when the child seems to have forgotten he was ever taught! But any time you put into training your children is time well spent, and it is time spent that prevents guilt later on—guilt that comes when your adult children are not trained to do what they are supposed to do, and guilt from knowing you have screamed and yelled at your children, losing any hope of ever being close. I want for you to have the joy of knowing you did your best in preparing your children for adulthood, and I also want you to have the joy of being close to your children!

I am not saying your children won't have difficulties as an adult. What I am saying is that I want you to have the confidence that you did your best to prepare your children for adulthood and that you did your best in trying to develop a close relationship with each of your children.

1.   **Realize that your children are not losers.** When your children repeatedly make the same mistake over and over, it is easy to begin feeling they are losers. However, if our children were perfect, there wouldn't be any use for us. They would not need parenting. Our children do need us, but that does not make them losers; it is simply the reason God gave children parents—to help train them in the various areas of their lives. And it takes different children different amounts of time to learn different tasks. Some tasks will come easier than others depending on the child's abilities and personality.

May I remind you at this point to not compare children to each other. You may think, "Well, Susie learned to make her bed at age two; Sally is five and still can't make her bed without wrinkles." That may be true, but Sally may be able to be friendly to people and make them feel good while

Susie is so shy she can't even say hello. Take children where they are and work to train them in each area at the pace they are able to learn.

2. **Realize God's plan for you is to train your children, so make plans as to how you will train them.** For example, help your children know that maintenance is going to take about three-fourths of their lives for the rest of their lives. Far too often, I think that we do too much for our children.

For instance, a schoolteacher will do all of the cleanup of the classroom at the end of the day. Her reasoning is that she should use class time to teach the children, and therefore must do the cleanup herself. Let me ask a question. Where do people have to spend most of their time? To me, it seems that most of a person's time is spent on cleanup and maintenance. Hair needs to be kept clean, styled, permed, cut, etc. Jewelry needs to be cleaned and maintained—a broken prong fixed, a loose diamond repaired, or a ring sized.

A car must be washed, vacuumed, have the oil changed, have mufflers replaced, and the engine tuned up. A yard must be raked, mowed, manicured, and fertilized. A house must be painted and maintained. Clothes must be washed, cleaned, repaired, and pressed. I could go on and on. Most of a person's time is spent on maintenance and cleaning if she has a successful life.

Yet, we seem to let our children out of cleanup and maintenance. Therefore, they don't understand what life is all about. If a class period is 50 minutes, about 35 to 40 of those minutes should be used to teach the subject matter. To really teach the children in a way that prepares them for life, the rest of the class period should be spent cleaning up and putting away things in an orderly manner. I think we do so much for the children that we don't teach them what they are going to have to do most of their lives.

At home, rather than being frustrated about the mess or the feeling that you have to do everything yourself, help the children be a part of cleanup and maintenance. For example, if you have very young children, each time they play with their toys, rather than allowing them to just dump all of their toys onto the floor, help them choose one or two toys with which to play. Then, when they want to change toys, help them know to put the first toys back in the toy box before they get out another set of toys. This training will teach them to clean and maintain their play area as they go.

As early as possible, have your children start assisting with chores such as doing the dishes and helping with the laundry. Let the children stack the dishes and get them ready to wash. Let the children help put away the dishes. Make it fun for your children to scrub the stains out of clothes before they are put into the washer. Make a game out of sorting the clothes by colors and types. Little children can be learning how to do laundry as they delight in putting whites in one pile, towels in a pile, and darks in another pile as you praise them and "ooh and ah" over their success.

Each time you get home from a trip or an errand, make it a practice to have the children help you pick up all the trash in the vehicle and take it to the garbage. Then have them look at the neat vehicle and praise them for their work. This routine is teaching them to maintain.

If your child's room looks like "the wreck of the Hesperus," don't start yelling and making such statements as, "This room is just a mess. I told you to clean it, and it still looks like a pig's sty!"

Rather, say something like, "Let's see how much we can get picked up in your room in the next ten minutes. When we are done, I have a treat for us." Then work with the child and praise every tiny bit of progress.

Dr. Don Boyd, principal of Hammond Baptist High School, often says, "Never criticize a child in an area where he is trying to learn." He teaches that criticizing stops the learning process. Dr. Boyd says instead to *praise* the child for any progress he makes in the area where he is trying to learn.

Remember, nurturing your child means training your child. Nurturing does not mean telling or yelling; it means patiently helping your child learn what he needs to learn to prepare him to be a successful adult.

Julie Boardway Richter is the daughter of Ray and Mabel Boardway and the wife of Brother Peter Richter. Ray and Mabel were young people at First Baptist Church of Hammond, Indiana, when Dr. Jack Hyles was called as pastor. Until a chronic illness caused him to resign, Brother Ray was the music director and chairman of the board of deacons at First Baptist Church for many years. Brother Pete is a deacon at First Baptist Church.

Julie is also the mother of two children. Having observed Julie while she was growing up and now watching her as a mother, I asked her several years ago about this matter of nurturing. I believe she was nurtured by her parents and is now nurturing her two children.

Julie said, "I have found there are certain times that cause me to become angry easily. I have a five-year-old boy who is full of energy. He is very outgoing and likes to have lots of fun. I have found that one time it is easy to get angry is when David has accidentally spilled something or knocked something over. The quick reaction is just to look at him and say, 'I can't believe you did that,' or 'Why did you do that when I just told you to set your glass by your plate?' Mine is a normal reaction.

"Just a couple of days ago, David knew I was going to be talking with you, so he helped me by giving me an example! We were eating supper, and he set his juice glass on the edge of his place mat. Of course, it spilled all over the table. I thought, 'I don't want to react because I have to tell those ladies the right way to do,' so I said, 'Now, David, let's get a towel.' We mopped up the juice, and then I said, 'This could be avoided if you will set the glass either on the place mat or on the table.' I showed him how to place the glass both ways, and he seemed to understand.

"I believe when we yell at our children or talk down to them, they feel belittled. In turn, belittling causes them to lose their self-confidence. We could instead nurture our children by showing them the right way to do certain tasks.

"Keep in mind that children are not going to learn a task right away or the first time you show them. David has spilled many things many times, so he doesn't have it yet. Repetition using patience and asking the Holy Spirit to help will enable us to nurture our children instead of react to the mistakes they make. When a child does something by accident, he simply needs his authority figure to patiently help him clean up the mess or correct the error and then once again be instructed as to how it could have been prevented or the right way to do the task."

I also asked Julie, "Have you ever found yourself reacting incorrectly to something one of your children does? If so, what do you do?"

Julie's response was, "Yes, unfortunately, I find myself reacting sometimes. When that happens I stop and think, 'You know this is not right.' Sometimes I react, and it is later when I think, 'Oh, I shouldn't have done that or said that.' I will go to my child and say, 'Mommy shouldn't have done what she did. I'm sorry I said what I did to you. Let me show you the way to do this.' Children seem to appreciate it when we recognize our wrong and apologize for mistreating them."

The Boardways have three daughters, all of whom seemed to have felt loved and accepted in their growing up years. Those daughters are now married, and two of them now have children. It seems to me that those children are happy, contented children. I believe the key is nurturing.

At the 2000 Thanksgiving service at First Baptist Church of Hammond, Brother Ray Boardway was honored for his years of service at First Baptist Church. As his daughters talked about their home life, it was evident there was a lot of fun, acceptance, and love, as well as a lot of nurturing when the Boardways patiently trained their girls.

Let me share some examples of nurturing and provoking:

Provoking

"No, you can't walk on the ledge."

Nurturing

"May I hold your hand while you walk on the ledge?"

"No, you may not go out in the rain!"

"Let's see if the neighbor kids can come over, and we'll all go out and play in the rain."

"No you can't go out in the lightning. It's too dangerous!"

"We can't go out in the lightning, but let's make a tent under the dining room table."

"You're just on that phone all the time. From now on you may never call your friends!"

"Let's figure out some rules that will give us all the right amount of phone time."

"Your room looks like the epicenter of an earthquake. I've never seen such a mess in my whole life!"

"Today when you get home, I'll have a snack ready, and we'll sit in your room while we eat and plan how to clean and decorate your room."

"You're a couch potato slob who does nothing but watch television!"

"Want to get your ball and bat and bike and go to the park with me?"

"It's about time you carried out the trash when I ask. You never obey!"

"You don't know how much I appreciate your carrying out the trash as soon as I asked."

"With those grades, you are going to flunk! I don't know why you can't get good grades!"

"Let me sit down in 15 minutes to see what you're doing on your homework. I'm so proud of you for working on it."

"You are so spoiled. You want everything. Don't you know we can't afford to give you everything you want?"

"From all the things you want, let's make a list showing in what order you most want them."

"I've told you before that it hurts my arm when I try to throw a ball with you. I can't go outside and play with you!"

"How about if we go ride bikes together?" or "Let's call Billy and see if he wants to play catch with you while I keep score."

You know, we parents even continue to provoke our children when they become adults. Let's look at some ideas on how to nurture our adult children.

Provoking

"I don't know why in the world you ever decided to become an air traffic controller! I'm disappointed you didn't go into the medical field."

Nurturing

"I don't know your line of work very well. Could you get me a book that would help me learn more about it?"

"I just can't seem to get gifts that please your wife. She never shows any appreciation for the gifts I buy her."

"What would be something I could give your wife for Christmas that she would like to have from me?"

"I am sorry you married Bill. He just doesn't fit into our family."

"Help me to know what Bill likes and enjoys. I want to be sure we include some of his interests while you are here visiting."

"You live so far away, and I hate the cold."

"What is the warmest time of the year in Alaska? Do you think Bob would be our personal tour guide if we planned to come for a few days in July?"

"You mean you are going to your in-laws for Christmas? We've always celebrated together as a family on Christmas day!"

"We will have our family Christmas whenever you get here; it's not a day—it's you we want."

Didn't you want nurturing and acceptance from your parents. Didn't you wish that just once you could make them happy? That is how your adult children feel when it seems they can never please you.

Now, guess who is going to eventually get the children at Christmas—the one who frees them. The parents who make the adult children feel free are the ones who will get the children. I have to admit that I was very bad about that. I wanted to go to my parents' home every Christmas, and we had to have a talk about it. I did need that talk, but never was it said to me by my in-laws that I was selfish about Christmas or anything like that. If they had talked that way, it probably would not have worked out the way it did. I would have gone to their house at Christmas, but I would have resented it.

Let me urge you, *nurture*—educate and train—rather than *provoke*—yell, scream, and belittle—your children!

I hate every memory of provoking my children; I love every memory of nurturing my children!

Dianne and Benny Dowdey

chapter five

℘arents: When You Don't Know What to Do

*Casey and Lisa Shearer with their children,
Michael, Matthew, Adam, Jacob, **Julia Marlene**,
and Leanna*

---

*"That our sons may be as plants grown up in their
youth; that our daughters may be as corner stones,
polished after the similitude of a palace."* (Psalms
144:12)

What a goal! To help our sons be mature in their
youth and to help our daughters be polished would take
great faith in the Lord and work, time, and study on our
part.

There was a time when you knew exactly what you needed or wanted to do at any given time. In fact, there was never enough time to do all that you were interested in doing. What happened? Could some type of trauma have entered your life? Trauma is an injury caused by an extrinsic agent such as an accident or surgery. Trauma results from emotional or mental injuries also. It could have been an emotional injury, such as a child running away from home, a child being in prison, a child announcing his or her "alternative lifestyle," or a child leaving a note saying he will never be back. There are so many hideous things worse than cancer and/or imminent death. How do you survive?

Keep Walking On!

Our preacher has said you get up, clean up, dress, and put one foot in front of the other. Wanting to do so has nothing to do with it. The only alternative is to lie around whining. That's the way down, and you won't enjoy that either. The fact is you just might not enjoy anything for months or years to come, depending on how or if a particular trauma is ever resolved. I'm not going to say you shouldn't cry, but that crying will probably come after the initial numbness wears off and should be done to God. He tells us over and over to pour out our complaints to him.

"I cried unto the LORD with my voice; with my voice unto the LORD did I make my supplication. I poured out my

complaint before him; I shewed before him my trouble."
(Psalms 142:1, 2)

"I cried unto thee, O LORD: I said, Thou art my refuge
and my portion in the land of the living." (Psalms 142:5)

Keep a Bible with You at All Times

"Who shall separate us from the love of Christ? Shall
tribulation, or distress, or persecution, or famine, or
nakedness, or peril, or sword? As it is written, For thy sake
we are killed all the day long; we are accounted as sheep for
the slaughter. Nay, in all these things we are more than
conquerors through him that loved us. For I am persuaded,
that neither death, nor life, nor angels, nor principalities, nor
powers, nor things present, nor things to come, Nor height,
nor depth, nor any other creature, shall be able to separate us
from the love of God, which is in Christ Jesus our Lord."
Romans 8:35-39 can help you as you gasp to get a breath.

In one of his sermons, our preacher emphasized the
words, "nor any other creature." He proposed the idea that
if there was anything missed in all that list of things which
cannot separate us from the love of Christ, the words, "nor
any other creature" cared for it.

The Bible might help you to realize the futility of trying
to understand the whys of that which has happened to you.
Following the four steps outlined in Proverbs 3:5 and 6
could keep you from "wallering" in your mess.

1. Trust in the Lord with all your heart.
2. Lean not to your own understanding.
3. In all your ways acknowledge Him.
4. He shall direct your paths.

The Bible can direct you to go soul winning. Winning a soul can so take your mind that you forget you're in the fight of your life—at least for a while.

The Bible can guide you to church. If you feel as if you can't fellowship with folks, slip in at the last minute, but go. Many times, just exactly what we need to hear is being preached and sung from the pulpit while we're at home wandering around the house trying to figure out what to do with ourselves.

The Bible can lead you to pray. Pray specifically rather than allowing prayer to be another way to continue your worries with a "Dear Lord" in front of it. Let another carry the prayer burden with you and for you.

You're on Your Way!

The difficult times will come. It seems that some of the greatest heartbreaks for a person are to see her own children suffering—whether it is from a chronic illness, an incurable disease, or worst of all, going into a life of sin and ruin. But the wonderful part is that God, in His love, has made ways for us to keep going when there is nothing we want to do. If you are following these steps, you are probably on your way.

chapter six

Circle the Wagons

*Jeannie Mae, K.W., and
Joe Carl Walker*

---

*"Enter into his gates with thanksgiving, and into his
courts with praise: be thankful unto him, and bless his
name."* (Psalms 100:4)

Play the "thankful game" in the car, at the table, or
waiting in a doctor's office at which time you see how
many things you can say or write for which you are
thankful today!

When Chelsea Clinton chose Stanford University as her college, one editorial I read said, "Stanford is circling the wagons, protecting their own as they have been known to do in the past. They will give very little information about the Clinton decision."

I thought that was a pretty good item of information. To think that the world would protect their own was rather startling to me.

In the trek to the West, "Circle the wagons!" was shouted out at the end of a day when cattle needed to be kept inside some kind of corral in order to be kept from straying. "Circle the wagons" was the cry when it was discovered that an Indian attack was imminent. "Circle the wagons" meant protection for their own.

Let's circle the wagons against bad television in all its forms. Let's circle the wagons against bad computer experiences and Internet access with all its ramifications. I am afraid we Christians are leaving too much space between wagons as far as the electronic world is concerned. We teach standards that would protect our children from worldliness and then let the world, in all its "glory," right into living rooms, family rooms, and bedrooms through electronic gadgetry. We plead ignorance in not knowing what all is involved with this fast-changing technological equipment, but we really aren't ignorant. We know the world is quick to pervert the use of any new invention. Before a new program is out of the production stage, the Devil has plans all mapped out for it. While we're pleading ignorance, any children for whom we are responsible are left unprotected. Let's circle the wagons.

Let's circle the wagons as far as keeping our mouths shut about our children. In this tell-all, talk-show age, we seem to feel as if we can give a daily rundown of our children's faults to each and every person with whom we come in contact.

It seems to me as if people used to think they had private lives which they worked out within the protective walls of their own family dwelling. In fact, if I remember right, people used to think there was no use in trying to get the "straight" of anything once they found out a possible suspect was protected by a family. Of course, this ideal was taken way too far—clear to the Mafia code. However, there must be a place of moderation between the philosophy of telling all at the drop of a hat and hiding your own—even if it means protecting a bomber.

Let's determine to circle the wagons around our children, nieces, nephews, grandchildren, church bus kids, Sunday school kids, neighbor kids, and the children of friends. Let's be a refuge (a sanctuary, if you please) to whom children can run for protection as we give them time to grow.

Rebekah and Elizabeth Hranicky

Elizabeth Vest

Kalyn Wilkie

chapter seven

My Child Is Overweight

Marlene Evans with Lauralee Gatto

———

"Bear ye one another's burdens, and so fulfil the law of Christ." (Galatians 6:2)

Those who work with children must help bear their burdens, which are to them too heavy.

———

"And this commandment have we from him, That he who loveth God love his brother also." (I John 4:21)

It's not an option; it's a commandment to love our brothers. We should teach and train our children to treat each other with love and respect.

Parents and those who work with teens, I beg you to take your larger child seriously. Please don't brush them off with statements such as, "Oh, you'll lose your baby fat." I still have "baby fat" at 67 years of age!

I plead with you not to talk and try to discuss with or make innuendoes about big people to your larger young people. I promise you they will only eat more of the wrong food. Yes, there are exceptions, but they are few and far between.

When I was in the seventh grade, I was as tall and as large boned as I am now. Really, I was not fat then, but being taller and larger boned than other kids was enough to make me feel humongous. It was also enough to give cause to my friends(?) for teasing me. It is a wonderful security to always have a place of refuge.

Someone once said, "Anything about which you get teased outside the refuge should be taboo inside the refuge." I had several refuges. I was okay at home—home safe! I was okay with Mom and Dad's close friends, "Aunt" Lela and "Uncle" Carl, who were both large people.

In fact, I was so okay that I felt I could share my hurt with them, and Aunt Lela responded with, "Marlene, when you're with Aunt Lela and Uncle Carl, you are with big people." As you can tell, I have never forgotten that empathy.

What Can You Do?

"So," you say, "what am I to do? My heart aches as I see my daughter or one of our teens getting bigger and bigger. It's ruining her whole life." Being a lady, I'm going to deal just with girls, although I know boys have many of the same problems.

Consider the Following Possibilities

• **Introduce her to Mrs. Beverly Hyles' cassette speaking tapes and books on feeling loved by God.** I do not know a slender, model-like lady any more able to relate to a large girl than Mrs. Hyles.

Tapes every girl should listen to are "Learning to Love Yourself," "You Are Somebody," and "Weight Control Tips to Help You Try One More Time." Books to read are *I Feel Precious to God* and *Marred Vessels in the Potter's Hand.*

• **Introduce her to Dr. Jack Hyles' tapes on the influence of a lady.** I do not know of a greater set of sermons or any kind of talks that could more help a girl want to become a lady who is so very important to God than the following six tapes:

"Needed, a Queen"	"Stay on Your Pedestal"
"Woman Power"	"Woman, the Completer"
"Woman, the Assembler"	"Woman, the Holy Spirit of the Home"

The materials listed above are available from *Christian Womanhood,* 8400 Burr Street, Crown Point, IN 46307.

• **Clothes are very important to help a bigger or out-of-proportion person feel better about themselves.** Man looks on the outward appearance according to I Samuel 16:7b which says, *"…for the LORD seeth not as man seeth; for man looketh on the outward appearance, but the LORD looketh on the heart."* Therefore, help your girl make extra money in order to be able to buy the clothes cut right for her. They probably will cost more, but they may make her look 10 to 15 pounds lighter. It is too bad the outward appearance means this much, but being somewhat of a realist, I have to admit it does. People seem to accept larger people better if they are dressed to look their best. How great it is that God accepts us just as we are!

It will take more time and effort to find the right styles to minimize size or a figure flaw. If your girl tries to go it alone, she might end up in tears of despair at the closest burger joint with french fries, a milk shake, an apple pie, and the burger, of course.

If you don't feel you are the one to help on such a shopping expedition, find someone who is, ask for their help, give them guidelines, and ask for veto power in order to return things after considering what is best for your child.

• *Get the book,* **Pattern for Living,** *which includes a whole unit explaining how to buy the right clothes to minimize each figure flaw a person may have.* This unit has been a great help to many in knowing how to dress in a way as to appear pounds thinner. (By the way, the fact that some people can put on a gunny sack and look good does not have to be mentioned!)

• *A flattering hairdo styled to draw attention toward the face and be in proportion to the larger body can be a real pain but can surely be easier than crying over the child's hurt feelings as she's talked against again and again.* Why spend time saying, "Kids are cruel," when we already know that the fact of cruelty has always been true and always will be on this earth. We're cruel, too!

• *Jewelry causes a lot of people to feel a little bit more normal no matter what the feelings of abnormality.* After my last surgery, my rings were brought to me within 24 hours. About 12 hours later, my ruby bracelet that had been at the jewelers being repaired was delivered to me. Miss Arlys Cooper went to Jeff at Jeffrey's Jewelers. He got the work out fast and free as a gift to me, and Miss Cooper sent the jewelry to Mayo Clinic with people who were coming to see me. I remember how good it felt to put on that bracelet. It is an expensive bracelet—a gift. However, I enjoy costume fun stuff, too.

• *Keep good snacks in the house or in a youth center or on an outing.* We yell at kids to lose weight and hand them a bag of chips, a soda, and a box of cookies. Be sure cut-up fruit and veggies, low-fat dips, strips of roast turkey or chicken, and other items are as available as junk food. **Say nothing. Do a lot.**

• *Provide good fun and fellowship.* If the girl about whom you are concerned is really overweight, you may have to provide most of the fun and fellowship she has. You can enlist help if you know the helpers are close-mouthed. If your girl ever knows she is a "project," you are a goner as far as helping her.

If you ever make your "big" child comfortable enough to talk to you and if I have been in your church or she to ours and if she likes me, you have my permission to tell her, "When you are around Mrs. Evans, you're around a big person." I'd like to think I could help another child or two.

The Darrell Hurst family

Michael Reeves

Cody Greenfield

chapter eight

My Friend Is No More Picky Than I Am!

Stephen, Simon and Samuel Cervantes (l-r)

———

"If any of you lack wisdom, let him ask of God, that giveth to all men liberally, and upbraideth not; and it shall be given him." (James 1:5)

Teach children to ask God for the wisdom they do not have.

———

"But be ye doers of the word, and not hearers only, deceiving your own selves." (James 1:22)

You and your children plan something to do that will immediately apply that which you have read in the Bible together.

My young preteen friend, who happens to be a boy, asked for an appointment to talk to me about getting over being picky. I told him I would not be a good one to ask about that as I have an opinion about everything.

Those of you who heard me give a speech at a Spectacular entitled "I'm Not Compatible with Anyone," know that I have preferences galore. Isn't it odd that most people don't call me picky but labeled a young boy with far fewer preferences as "picky."

Now I understand it could be that I have refused to make my preferences known in such a pronounced way as to look startled and start shaking when I see something on the table I don't like. It also could be that I eat a little of everything and make no pronouncements on food I don't like, but I have *taste* upon top of tastes.

Food isn't the most important thing at a time of getting together with family or friends. ***The people are the important part of the gathering.*** Some of us actually have thought that the food was the most important part!

In trying to help my friend, I tried to relate to him (not difficult), unlabeled him (his parents said they'd take the word "picky" out of their vocabulary), and tried to teach him what he could do to expand his food taste range and to please his hostesses.

The following were the notes I brought to my appointment with my young friend.

My Friend Is No More Picky Than I Am!

1. You are not picky.
2. You have tastes as I do.
3. It is all right to have tastes.
4. It is also right to try to like every good thing.
5. It is also right to be thankful for someone trying to do something for you whether or not you like it.
6. It is also right to be quiet about your dislikes.

Please join me in treating a kid as well as or better than you do an adult. *"...Jesus said, Suffer little children, and forbid them not, to come unto me: for of such is the kingdom of heaven."* (Matthew 19:14)

Rebekah and Sarah Wruck

Cori (l) and Cassidy Lindsey

The Chris Wheeler family

$\mathscr{A}$ Lifetime Challenge for the Gifted

Alexander Carver

"Thou shalt teach them diligently unto thy children, and shalt talk of them when thou sittest in thine house, and when thou walkest by the way, and when thou liest down, and when thou risest up." (Deuteronomy 6:7)

Take walks with your children. Exercising and observation skills can be learned while memories are made away from responsibilities and the telephone.

We are hearing a lot about providing a challenge for the gifted in the way of enrichment programs and special classes. The thinking seems to be that the gifted who do not receive this help will get bored in the home, school, and church and will get into trouble. I'm sure it is fine to enrich the curriculum or activities for the gifted as well as for anyone of any ability.

I do, however, question the term "gifted." In what way are we speaking? Usually we presume that we are discussing the academically gifted. Sometimes there are those who appear to be gifted academically, musically, and athletically. Whether a student is gifted in one area or several areas, I do believe there is a way to keep your child challenged, and anything but bored, without having the wherewithal to put him into a ghetto situation of gifted only.

The way I am suggesting to help the gifted would give him the opportunity of being gifted in people skills. He will not function well in life no matter how many gifts he has if he cannot find a way to relate to all kinds of people.

In trying to think of work that does not take people skills, I am at a loss. A piano tuner or research person might work alone, but he still has to communicate with employers, and, of course, he needs to have an enriched family life. There is no way to be a good Christian without working to win or help people. People are the Christian's business.

My suggestion: Teach a gifted child to be "apt to teach." "*And the servant of the Lord must not strive; but be gentle unto all men, apt to teach, patient."* (II Timothy 2:24)

The academically gifted will spend a lifetime around those of lesser ability. No two minds are alike. How could your gifted person ever get bored patiently teaching and helping those around him?

The Jim Beller family

Heather Tefft

Bekah Williamson

chapter ten

Your Child vs. Bullies

*Katie, Jenny, and Joshua
Hedderman*

"Let nothing be done through strife or vainglory; but in lowliness of mind let each esteem other better than themselves." (Philippians 2:3)

Be sure to give a good hearing to your child's suggestions.

If your child has lost his confidence because of being bullied, he is the only one who can get it back. You cannot get it back for him by talking to school authorities, students, parents, or your friends. You might have to talk to a school authority, but that in itself will do nothing to empower your child for a lifetime of handling bullies.

He must be guided to accept (whether or not he understands) the fact that there will be bullies in his way all life long. Just as soon as one bully is out of the way, another one appears as if he has been waiting in the wings ready to make life miserable.

Instead of crying, wringing your hands, and sympathizing, how about getting your child ready to face bullies spiritually, emotionally, mentally, and/or physically.

1. **Help him understand that people who want to do evil to others are as old as the Bible.** Read the story of Joseph with him to show how Joseph turned out to have his brothers' fates in his hands. *"And Joseph said unto them, Fear not: for am I in the place of God? But as for you, ye thought evil against me; but God meant it unto good, to bring to pass, as it is this day, to save much people alive. Now therefore fear ye not: I will nourish you, and your little ones. And he comforted them, and spake kindly unto them."* (Genesis 50:19–21)

Read Psalms with him to show what happens in God's time to evildoers.

Use other Bible stories such as David and Saul.

2.   **Role play.** You be the bully and surprise him by tripping your child physically or verbally. Teach him how to think, what to say or not say, and how to go on as if nothing happened when that is appropriate.

3.   **Take your child's need to look a little bit "in" seriously.** Help your child dress in clothes that are fashionable, that fit properly, and that are good styles and colors for him. This is not an area in which to save money by using love gifts, hand-me-downs, or bargains that were not purchased with your child in mind. This is an area over which you *do* have some control. A bargain is only a bargain if it helps your child look his best and helps give him the type of confidence that stylish, well-fitting clothes can give. I wish this were not so important, but the fact is, it is.

4.   **Teach him how to defend himself and his family.** If you believe in martial arts, ask a Christian who knows some karate or other self-defense skill to teach your child. I use this point, hoping he never has to use his techniques. Many times just the knowledge that he has the ability will help restore his confidence.

I used the pronoun "he" throughout this chapter but full well know there are as many girls being bullied as boys. I also know bullying goes on in Christian schools as well as public schools and in fundamental Sunday school classes and youth groups just as in liberal churches.

5.   **Enlist the help of resource people who will not get bent out of shape but can help you in your campaign to get your child suited up for the battle of life.** Be sure they know any talk against the bully is a waste of their breath.

Saved kids are going to Heaven when they die, but they may be very carnal Christians who have had little character or compassion training.

In a Christian school, you have a much better chance of a principal or teacher stopping the outward bullying of your child. However, the bully can go underground in a meaner way.

We live in an imperfect world with imperfect people. Perfection is what Heaven is for!

chapter eleven

Every Child Is a Problem Child

Marlene Evans with Chad Dowdey

"Let your moderation be known unto all men. The Lord is at hand." (Philippians 4:5)

Helping a child to go to bed before he is exhausted, to stop playing before he gets angry with his playmates, to quit eating before he is stuffed, etc., will cause him to be happy as he knows how to control himself in more and more areas of his life.

"Rejoice in the Lord alway: and again I say, Rejoice." (Philippians 4:4)

Helping a child to give his hurts to God will help him become a victorious Christian.

One of the best kept secrets from moms is the fact that *every* child is a problem child. This secret surely must be a trick of the Devil since there is so much Scripture to help us know that every child is a problem child. In fact, we adults are just grownups still fighting problems we had as children. This fact is proven in Scripture.

"There is none that understandeth, there is none that seeketh after God." (Romans 3:11)

"Behold, I was shapen in iniquity; and in sin did my mother conceive me." (Psalms 51:5)

"As it is written, There is none righteous, no, not one." (Romans 3:10)

"For all have sinned, and come short of the glory of God." (Romans 3:23)

We give lip service to the knowledge that each child just has a different set of strengths and weaknesses, and each child comes ready to be trained and tempered by parents. Then, we get an "angel" amongst our children—often one who is quiet and polite and presents few *outward* problems to parents or friends. Sometimes the "angel" is a cute child full of personality—you know, the one no one can resist.

I feel more sorry for these "angels" than I do for the labeled "problem" child. The problem child is sometimes noisy, awkward, and destructive; and he tells everything that pops into his mind. The old saying, "What you see is what you get," holds true here. The parents, everyone in the store, and each church goer sees and/or complains loudly and long about the problem child, which tends to brainwash a parent into thinking the "angel" who gives so little trouble needs little help.

Because of this pressure from friends to clean up the act of the problem child, he often gets more help, time, and discipline while the other one quietly seethes and waits to get revenge.

Allow me to give just two examples from my years in teaching and Christian work.

A family who had two girls were blessed very definitely with an "angel" and a problem child. The problem child caused no real havoc but was ornery, thereby causing adults all kinds of discomfort. She questioned all the rules of life, and, in general, caused adults to feel uncomfortable. This discomfort often came as a result of not being able to answer the questions, not being able to admit they couldn't answer the questions, and therefore, not knowing how to help the child find the answers.

The "angel" never asked any questions and was a sweet, polite girl who was greatly admired by the older ladies of the church. The problem girl found her way to get answers; the "angel" didn't need any answers in the minds of the adults in her life.

Today the sweet girl is married to an unsaved man going the way of the world and training her children to do the same. They are what the world would call good citizens. The problem girl has been married to a fine Christian man who, with her help, has worked with Christian young people for years and years. A scenario such as this doesn't have to work out this way, but far too often it does.

A young lady of my acquaintance was a joy to rear,

requiring little time, discipline, or tempering from her parents throughout her days at home. She lived in her room studying, typing, sewing, and making crafts. She now has been out of her home for more years than she lived in her parental home. By her own admission, as well as from observation, I can safely say she has spent every day of her adult life "paying back" her folks for not getting her out of her room once in a while and getting to know her particular set of problems.

God gives parents, preachers, teachers, and adult friends to help each child in the way he needs it—not to enjoy or dislike them as we label them. Look at each of the children in your care—whether it is your own children, children you teach in a classroom, children you babysit, or relatives with whom you visit. As you look at each of these individual children, try to assess what needs they may have.

• If the child is quiet and seems content to be alone all the time, help the child take "baby steps" toward interacting with other children.

• If the child is shy, help the child learn to talk appropriately to other people by practicing what to say when she comes in contact with others.

• If the child is bossy, help her know how to blend and let others sometimes choose what game they will play.

• If the child is clumsy, help the child learn to operate a little more slowly in order to not spill milk at every meal.

Let's help the children!

chapter twelve

Tempering Your Child

Jonathan, Jessica, David and Chuckie Condict

———

"He looketh on the earth, and it trembleth: he toucheth the hills, and they smoke." (Psalms 104:32)

Spend time with your child just quietly watching a lake, the sky, or a mountain, pointing out the differences as the sun shifts and as birds or animals make their appearances.

———

"And, ye fathers, provoke not your children to wrath: but bring them up in the nurture and admonition of the Lord." (Ephesians 6:4)

When leaving the house with small children, take a bag of favorite toys, books, and games since they cannot plan ahead for time periods they do not understand.

As a child, I used to hear about a man who was referred to as a "prince of a man." That meant he was balanced—he was gentle; he was kind; he was a hard worker; he was honest. That's what we want our children to be. Jesus left us the ultimate example in Luke 2:52, *"And Jesus increased in wisdom and stature, and in favour with God and man."* Jesus was balanced.

It doesn't mean we want young people to be "highfalutin', high muckety-muck royalty." It means we want them to be good people. How is that going to happen?

Kids are not just dropped down on us as bad or good. We're all bad. We all come out of the womb as sinners. Psalms 58:3a says, *"...they go astray as soon as they be born, speaking lies."* So all kids are bad; all kids need tempering; all kids need help.

We adults all have areas where we need to become more tempered. We actually could take these points I am going to give about children and apply them to our own lives to help us in the areas where we need tempering. We all have weaknesses on which we will have to work for the rest of our lives.

I have observed a few families in which it seems the children are happy and obedient and where it seems that the parents are really working to help those children become balanced in their personalities. In talking with these families, I find that people say to the parents, "You surely are fortunate to have children like these," as those people watch the children obey so beautifully in public. No, those families are not fortunate. Those parents have worked themselves to death.

I know of a case where someone said to a mother about her first child, who was so beautifully mannered (and all boy too), "I don't know if you'll get another one like that." No, they won't, because they didn't *get* that one. Good marriages, good children, or good relationships aren't dropped on us.

People seem to think that those who have happy marriages or well-adjusted, obedient children just had this wonderful situation dropped from Heaven. Wouldn't that be great if that was the case? Believe me, I think that would be tremendous. But it just doesn't happen.

Let me reiterate that even the children you think are trained more easily and seem as if they are better children are usually just quieter children. I have discovered these quieter children simply go underground with their wrong behavior. A quieter child is still a sinner, so he is not perfect. In fact, it scares me to see quieter children. It seems that Sunday school teachers, grandparents, and most everybody likes that quieter child while they have no idea what that quieter child's needs are. Therefore, the quieter child may never get help with his areas of weakness.

Romans 3:23 says, *"For all have sinned, and come short of the glory of God."* A quiet child is a sinner, and a loud child is a sinner. All children are sinners, and it is up to us to help the children in our care to become more tempered in their personalities.

Maybe you are saying, "Oh, I wish I would have done something differently in rearing my children so my kids could be happier and have better, richer lives." I am not writing this chapter to make anyone feel guilty. There are things all of us wish we had done differently. If you have adult children who are not living for the Lord or are unhappy and unfulfilled, just try to figure out what you can do now. I discuss this in more detail in the chapter, "Child-Rearing Traps to Avoid." Especially study child-rearing trap number 10 to help you with your adult children. But let me urge you not to spend your time thinking on your regrets. I want to help you find solutions.

Proverbs 22:6 says, *"Train up a child in the way he should go: and when he is old, he will not depart from it."* Do you know that *train* does not mean *spank*? It might be a part of training, but that is not the main teaching of this verse. We are supposed to spank our children, and we are given very clear instructions to do so in the Bible. However, *train* is different from yelling at, screaming at, spanking, lecturing or any of this. *Training is directing growth.*

Somehow we seem to feel as if, "Oh, that boy is a sissy, and there's nothing anyone can do about it." or "That girl is just loud and bossy, and there's nothing I can do about it."

There is something we can do about it, no matter what personality trait seems to be extreme in a child. In fact, we are commanded to do something about it. We are to train and redirect the personality growth of that child. What can you do with your own children or children under your care to help them become more tempered in their personalities?

Certainly within this chapter I cannot cover every personality trait I have ever noticed. However, perhaps the following suggestions will present some ideas of ways you can help direct the growth of the children in your care to help them become balanced, obedient, happy adults.

TEMPERING A SISSY BOY. I believe two obvious traits about sissy boys label them and cause them to be ridiculed—effeminate gestures with their hands and dainty, unmanly steps.

My husband has a farmer's walk; he grew up as a farmer. I've known my husband to be out in front of his office in the hallway at Hyles-Anderson College helping young men learn to walk in a more masculine way by taking long, big strides. I don't know whether they want his particular walk or not, but it sure is better than the little mini-steps the young men have been taking.

Teachers or leaders who are all upset about an effeminate boy are too often a part of making fun of that boy rather than making progress by helping the boy know how to walk in a masculine way or getting him to someone who can help him.

TEMPERING A TOMBOY. Don't put her in frills. That would be too much. We think we will frill 'em out, lace 'em up, and put all this jewelry and stuff on them to make them feminine. You know they hate it, and it only makes them all the more want to go toward boy things.

Promote girl clothes, and promote some of that "girl interest" but don't go completely overboard making her wear things you wouldn't want to wear yourself. There are only a few people who look good in frills and lace and all that kind of stuff, so you don't have to go that extreme.

I was so pleased one day when I heard about a little girl (who has the possibilities of being a confirmed tomboy) receiving a great compliment. As I thought about it, I wondered if the compliment couldn't belong in part to a mom, a dad, an aunt, and several other people whom God has placed in that child's life.

Instead of constantly getting after the little girl for being "tomboyish," and labeling the girl to herself and others, the mom takes her to garage sales and dollar stores to buy ribbons, barrettes, feminine dresses, beads, and bracelets. Her dad watches every opportunity to praise her feminine look. An aunt made her a pair of culottes (that looked like a skirt in the front and back) when she began to crawl. The same aunt has gone to great lengths to make her niece feminine (but not overly dressy) dresses for school and church.

This little girl has times she's encouraged to run, jump and climb trees, but she is gaining great grounds at being appropriate and feminine.

Oh, the compliment I heard: "It looks like she's having fun being a girl!"

TEMPERING A SHY CHILD. At ladies' meetings I have often had the women bow their heads after which I ask, "How many of you were shy as a child?" Dozens of hands are raised. Then I ask, "How many of you wish you had gotten help as a child and still suffer to this day from shyness?" Many of those same hands are raised.

It is tempting when a timid child hides behind Mommy's dress and doesn't respond to a hello from someone for the mother to speak up and say, "Susie's shy," and think that takes care of it.

It doesn't! It is not helping that child learn to go outside of herself and be polite to people. It is giving that child an excuse for not speaking to people and causing her to be thought of as rude or "uppity" for the rest of her life.

Practice at home with a young child who is shy. Play the part of another adult and help the child know how to respond to different questions she might be asked. For example, "Hi, what is your name?" Help the child look in your eyes and say clearly, "Susie." "How old are you, Susie?" Have the child look in your eyes and say clearly, "I am three."

It will take time, but you are tempering that child and helping her for the rest of her life. Maybe you are a natural talker and so you don't even relate to this, but realize that for a shy person, words come slowly. They oftentimes don't even know what words to say. Practice at home before they go visit relatives. *Patiently* practice, practice, and practice some more so the child never feels your frustration but does have confidence to look people in the eyes and greet them and answer their questions.

TEMPERING A LOUD CHILD. Often the loud child can come across as bossy. Just as you practice with the shy child, helping her know how to speak to people, you will practice with the loud child. Help the outgoing child learn to let others choose what the group plays. Help the outgoing child learn to rephrase statements to make them less hurtful. For example, if your loud child says to a sibling, "I want to play with Legos now," ask, "Mary, how can you say that in a kinder way?" Help her to say to her brother, "Would it be okay with you if we play Legos now?"

TEMPERING A PRISSY GIRL. I am talking about someone who is so feminine she is almost sickening. There are little girls who can't do anything. They sit really still and can never do anything for fear they might get dirty.

Help her do some things such as plant some flowers in

a pot, wash a garbage can, etc. to help her become more balanced.

TEMPERING A CHILD WHO EXAGGERATES. Some children do exaggerate the truth. They actually see things bigger than they are, but most people view them as liars. I can relate to this because I know I have the capability within my personality to exaggerate.

My mother had a birthday party for me when I was a kindergarten child in a tiny town of Nebraska. I doubt that there were 90 kids in the entire school, but I told people there were 90 kids at our house for my party. The house was tiny, the town was tiny, the school was tiny, and there were not 90 kids at my house. There might have been nine, but I had never had nine in my house before, and I really felt there were 90 people there.

I know that I feel things bigger than they are. My dad went to be with the Lord in 1998, but before he passed away, I used to call him and check my stories with him. I didn't trust whether or not I was remembering things bigger than they really were. You can ask kids questions to help them to begin to check on themselves.

TEMPERING A CHILD WHO COMPLAINS. A complaining child may say, "I never get what I want." You might respond with, "You *never* get what you want?" Help that child face what he is saying and thinking. You might ask, "Last week after school what did you get to do?"

When the child answers, say, "Now was that what you wanted to do? Did you choose that? Then is it true that you never get what you want?" Help the child see that sometimes he does get to do what he wants to do—about 25 times a day, in fact!

It is tempting to make remarks like, "I give you what you want all the time...you just don't appreciate all you get...etc., etc." But giving him a big lecture will not help. Just calmly help him be able to face facts and see that he does get to do some of what he wants.

TEMPERING A CHILD WHO POUTS. Pouting is showing outward displeasure with the events of life. What if you said to a kid when he's pouting, "I feel badly that you are having such a hard time. What could we do to get that smile back on your face? I'd like to see you happy."

Most kids are not going to say, "Take me to Disney World!" For most children, it's pretty simple. I've asked girls all over the country to tell me what they most like to do with their mothers. One of them just recently said, "What I most like that my mother ever did for me was take off work when I was sick at home; she went and got crackers for me." Now, that's pretty typical of the responses I get. Children are not as greedy as we act like they are. What most of them really want is us. They want us to care about them. We might find that if we did something they want, like get some crackers, we'd make a memory that would be way beyond a Disney World experience.

TEMPERING A CHILD WHO HAS A SMART MOUTH. Sometimes I say some pretty harsh things. I'm not even feeling that badly about the situation, but what I say just comes out harshly. I say often, "Let me rephrase that."

We need to help our children start rephrasing some things. We do need to let them express themselves, but it is important *how* they express themselves. All that stuff the world is saying about, "Just let them say what they want to say any way they want to say it" is just plain wrong. But we often go to the other extreme, and sometimes we don't have a clue about what is bothering our children. They know they can't tell Mom because Mom will have a fit. We had better be knowing what they are thinking. So help them know how to tell you what is on their minds.

TEMPERING A CHILD WHO IS FEARFUL. Maybe you have a child who won't stay in the nursery or a Sunday school class without a big fuss because of fear. Make times to be away from that child for very short periods. Then return when or before you said you would return so they get a sense of trust in you. When you leave them in Sunday school or in the nursery, be on the back row in church so you are the first parent in line for your child. This will help you build a sense of trust with the child.

What about an older teen who is fearful? Teach her that she might be left alone sometimes. She might be left alone at an activity where nobody seems to want to be with her. Get her ready to find someone else who seems to be alone and become a friend to that person. Help her know what to do if she's left alone. Talking through different scenarios will help the fearful teen know what might happen and how she can handle the situations.

TEMPERING A CHILD WHO DOESN'T SEEM TO FOLLOW THROUGH ON A JOB OR GETS SIDETRACKED. A young teen and her family were helping me get some things for the Ryders, my "young'uns" home from the mission field at Christmastime. I asked the teen to get a particular item in Wal-Mart. She came back with several other things but not the item I had asked her to get. She told me she thought maybe I would like to see these other things because she felt they would be good for my family.

Her mother talked with me a short time later because the girl was having the same trouble in school. People were saying of her, "She won't follow instructions."

So now her mother is going to stores like Wal-Mart quite often and sending the girl across the store for one thing. If she doesn't bring that one thing back, the mother asks her to go again and get that one thing. After the girl learns to go get one thing and only do that one thing, the mother will help her learn to go get two things.

TEMPERING A CHILD WHO WANTS TO LEAD RATHER THAN FOLLOW. I was out riding my bicycle with some young people one day, and a five-year-old would not follow the leader. The next thing I knew that boy's mother was out on a bike with that five-year-old behind her. She was teaching him to follow the leader. She didn't give a lecture, and she didn't spank him. She just went out alone with him and taught him to follow the leader on a bicycle. That was beautiful to me because I just don't see that type of training happening much. What that mother did was direct growth.

There are many other areas too numerous to discuss in this chapter where our children need tempering. Watch your children, and find these areas. Don't make statements such as, "I just wish I didn't have a fearful child," or "I was never fearful. Why is my child fearful?" or "My other kids aren't fearful." Rather, use that time thinking of creative ways to help direct the growth of your children in that area or any other area.

I am not saying we are to change our children. We simply want to help them add to their personalities. We want to direct their growth just a little bit at a time.

I want to see women be used to help children become

balanced in their lives. I want us to be patient, kind, and loving to bus kids, Christian school kids, nieces, nephews, grandchildren, and our own children. We are needed so badly. I think I can help some kids. What about you?

chapter thirteen

Child-Rearing Traps to Avoid

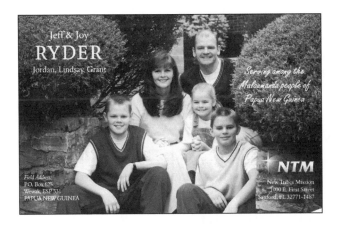

"Look not every man on his own things, but every man also on the things of others." (Philippians 2:4)

Sometime really look at your child when she is talking to you.

———

"A merry heart maketh a cheerful countenance." (Proverbs 15:13a)

Enjoy a swing yourself when taking your children to the park. Play in the sand with your child rather than only watching. Smile and laugh with your child.

It seems that once people have reared their children, they look back and wish they had not fallen into certain traps. Now, children don't like for their parents to tell what they might have done wrong in child rearing, because it implies that possibly the children are the scoundrels of the earth. How often have you heard an adult child say, "Oh, Mom, don't tell that!"

So, in order for me to keep from embarrassing my children, I am not telling whether these child-rearing traps are ones I did or did not avoid. The traps I am discussing in this chapter are ones that I have observed through the years.

CHILD-REARING TRAP #1
Overreacting to Some Parenting We Received

You've heard it, and you've probably thought it—"I had to work so much as a child, and I resented it. I'm going to see to it my child doesn't have to work that much." These types of thoughts cause parents to swing to the other side of the pendulum, and the end result is that their children don't learn to work. Parents' overreaction to having to work hard as children robs their own children of the character that is taught in learning to work; it robs their children of knowing the joy and satisfaction of a job well done; and it robs their children of a sense of accomplishment and the knowledge of how to do a job right.

Parents also make statements such as , "I'm going to see

to it that my child has good clothes. I didn't have very nice clothes when I went to school, and I felt so humiliated." Our overreaction causes us to go overboard and see to it that our child has a designer outfit for every day of the month. That, in turn, causes her to be resented by her classmates because she has so many clothes.

Another statement might be, "My parents told me they'd give me an allowance, and by the time I was supposed to get the allowance they would always tell me what I'd done wrong. I didn't get any money. I'm going to see to it that my boy has money to jingle all the time." Now don't get me wrong, I think that a boy needs some money to jingle in his pocket. But giving a child an excessive amount of money spoils him and does not prepare him for adulthood.

Be careful of overreacting to some parenting you feel you received. Even if you love your folks dearly, and even if you think they did a pretty good job, there are still some thoughts which will come to your mind about which you feel your parents didn't do quite right in some way. However, if you do overreact and swing completely the other way on the pendulum, you are very likely going to do a bad thing also, and your children will be saying, "I'm not going to do what my parents did."

Keep Philippians 4:5 in mind to help you with this child-rearing trap. *"Let your moderation be known unto all men. The Lord is at hand."*

CHILD-REARING TRAP #2
Making Excuses for Bad Behavior

When a child is throwing a tantrum, it is so easy to excuse that behavior because of various reasons such as, but not limited to, "He is teething." "She has an earache." "He is tired." "She had her shots today." or "She's hungry."

According to some parents, there is always a reason why their child is acting badly. Once parents start making excuses for a child's disagreeable behavior, that child is going to grow up thinking that if she is sick, if she is tired, or if she has some other difficulty, she can act any way she wants. However, Proverbs 20:11 teaches, *"Even a child is known by his doings, whether his work be pure, and whether it be right."* Therefore, the time to train a person to behave properly and appropriately in every situation is when she is a child.

Children will feel better—even if they are teething, have an earache, or are tired—if a parent will help get them in control of themselves and calmed down.

Take care of the problem as soon as possible. Put the tired child to bed; get medicine for teething pain; take the sick child to the doctor; feed the hungry child.

There are times when it is appropriate to spank a child in the midst of his frustration. Sometimes a child is so tired that he can't go to sleep. More than once I have seen a parent give an overly tired child a little spanking and seen the child go to sleep in seconds.

This is a difficult task. It is hard enough to spank the child for disobedience when he seems to be feeling well, and it is doubly hard to spank when there are extenuating circumstances such as sickness. In addition to that, the world is screaming that spankings equal child abuse. But a little spanking right square on the bottom will settle the child and will give her a better night's sleep as the child realizes she is going to have to calm down.

It doesn't matter what the cause. Possibly you are feeling to blame because you carted the child around the mall for hours without food or a nap. (We've all seen children in the mall who are falling all over each other because they are so tired. They are whining and crying and the mother says, "I just want to go into one more store," and then proceeds to continue through the entire mall. You see the same mother and her children an hour later with the children still whining, and still crying, and the mother stating she just wants to visit one more store!) Even if you are at fault, something needs to be done; the child needs to be brought under control. Often, a little spanking will help the child settle down and go to sleep.

It's not fun. In fact, there is a lot about child rearing that is not pleasant. Much of what we have to do as parents is pretty hard. Cleaning dirty diapers, spanking our children, or getting up in the middle of the night when a child has the stomach flu are not activities we really want to do.

Back in the days when I was in band, we had to practice the same songs over and over. It wasn't very much fun. All the sour notes were pointed out by the band director, and then we would have to play the songs over and over again. How many times I heard, "Let's go back to this bar of the music," or "Let's start at the beginning." Most of it wasn't fun. But the night we performed the concert for our parents and friends we sounded so good, and *that* was a lot of fun.

Most of our fun in rearing children is going to come years from now. Oh, there are some good times right now—when the baby coos, when a child does new things, or when he laughs and smiles. I don't want to make child-rearing sound terrible, or spread gloom or doom, but I do want to help you understand that child rearing does include many unpleasant responsibilities.

One of those unpleasant times is having to face the difficulties, whatever they may be, and helping the child act in a right way through hard times rather than making excuses for wrong behavior.

CHILD-REARING TRAP #3
Not Spanking the Baby Until He Understands

Of course, I realize that child abuse is a major problem today. Parents are abusing children by breaking bones and slapping them across their ears and eyes and that type of thing. But, please, don't let the fact that some people abuse children cause you to give up what the Bible says in Proverbs 13:24, *"He that spareth his rod hateth his son: but he that loveth him chasteneth him betimes."* Proverbs 19:18 says, *"Chasten thy son while there is hope, and let not thy soul spare for his crying."*

Oh, how often I wanted to quit when I was in the middle of a spanking. Children can cry so pitifully as if their heart is broken in two. Some children don't seem to need as much spanking as others. Their heart really is broken, they sincerely repent, and they don't commit that particular offense again. Others seem to know just how to tear your heart out with their crying, so you stop, only to have to spank again later because the matter was not settled. A parent must get to know his children and their responses to spankings.

No matter how much a child has cried and repented, if he immediately commits the same offense, the parent has not finished the spanking. (I don't mean that sometime later the child might not do the same thing. I am referring to the times when the minute you stop spanking the child goes right back to doing the same thing for which he was disciplined.) When that happens, you can be assured the child did not get the message. You didn't spank hard enough or long enough to get through, no matter how much the child cried. Don't let your soul spare for his crying. Proverbs 29:15 teaches, *"The rod and reproof give wisdom: but a child left to himself bringeth his mother to shame."*

Some people say we should not spank until the time a child can understand. It has been said that time is when the child is a year old, whereas some people insist a child understands as early as nine months. Other people believe that the age of understanding comes when the child is more than a year old; still others say it is when the child begins crawling or walking.

I say don't spend a lot of time worrying and agonizing over this matter. If you are just tapping and stinging a little bit on the child's bottom with your hand, it is not going to hurt him. The truth is we don't know when a child understands.

Now, I am not saying that you should spank the child the first night he is home from the hospital, or in the first few weeks or months of life. I am talking about when that child looks at you and goes right ahead and does something he should not do. Children are able to do that pretty early in life. They know a lot more than we think they know, even at nine months. They are pretty sharp little creatures. I would rather give a few spanking before they understand than let them go through a few months understanding when

I didn't give the spankings.

If you are going to err, why don't you err on the side that would be the best biblically? Don't worry about what people say. People who criticize parents for spanking their children generally don't produce happy, obedient children. Don't even listen to anything on the radio or television and don't read secular helps on child rearing.

Read and study the Bible to learn about child rearing. As I mentioned before, keep in mind Proverbs 22:6 which says, *"Train up a child in the way he should go: and when he is old, he will not depart from it."* If you look up every cross reference for that verse, you will be surprised. People have told me that doing this study has caused them to check out several hundred verses.

It is the Devil's trap for you to think you should not spank because you fear the child will not understand. A small child can understand "No!" and a smack on the hand when he plays with a glass dish. Let the Bible give you confidence to spank your child when he is young and can learn quickly.

CHILD-REARING TRAP #4
Believing that Love and Praise Will Spoil the Child

How many times have you heard someone say, "You are going to spoil that baby!" to a parent who is loving on a baby?

How is our love and praise going to spoil the child? Love and praise are going to make a child feel accepted and confident so he can go ahead and start leaving the parents' arms as he toddles off to another room. Love and praise are going to make a child feel accepted and confident so he can someday leave his parents' house and walk to the neighbor's house. Love and praise are going to make a child feel accepted and confident so he can someday walk away and go to school, go to a job, go to college, and eventually get married.

Love and praise are not going to spoil that child. What spoils a child is giving that child his way. A parent can even give a lot of things to a child without spoiling that child if he doesn't give him what he wants when he wants it upon demand. I don't think it's probably a good idea to give children lots of things they don't need or possibly that they don't even want. (You know how you've put all those tricycles, bicycles, and scooters together only to watch the child go play with the box!) We could give children simpler things, and they would be just as happy (while they would also learn a little bit about getting along with less). Still, you can give things and not spoil a child.

You can rock the child a lot and love on him. You can trace his little fingers and toes and thank God for that little baby. That won't spoil a child.

People have heard so many times that love spoils a child, they feel like, "Oh, I shouldn't tell my children good things I think about them." I have heard people say, "I'm not going to say too much good about her because if I do I might spoil her."

Now, the fact is, you don't want to go around excessively bragging on every little thing your child does. Bragging on the child and making big over every tiny little thing he does can cause him to question whether or not you really think he's good because he has to do so little to be bragged on.

But do praise the child's character, and do tell the child you love him, and do touch the child and demonstrate your love. Loving your child and praising him will not spoil him!

CHILD-REARING TRAP #5
Overcompensating for Special, Difficult, or Unfortunate Circumstances

It is so easy for a parent to overcompensate because of a child's sickness, or because the parents waited such a long time for the baby, or because the parents have a hectic schedule and don't have much time for the child, or because the mother works outside the home.

Some parents overcompensate in a wrong way by buying the child an excessive amount of toys, clothes, food, or other things. Other parents overcompensate by letting the child have his way. Oftentimes parents do these things to alleviate their own guilt.

First of all, doing these things will not alleviate the guilt. Secondly, doing these things will hurt the child and give him unrealistic expectations for adulthood.

The answers lie in finding the root of the problem and making some adjustments. For example, if you work outside the home, you probably are not going to be able to do much extra if you have children. Women often say to me, "I work a job outside the home; I have four children; I teach a Sunday school class; I help my husband on his church bus route; I am in the church choir. How can I get it all done?" My answer is simple as I say, "You can't."

Realize that you are not a superwoman. Let your husband help you know your priorities, and what responsibilities you should accept. Then say "no" to other seeming opportunities and responsibilities.

Cindy Schaap tells that her father once told her when she was faced with the opportunity to travel and speak, "Opportunities come around again; relationships don't." Cindy wisely realized that her children would only grow up one time.

When you are asked to take on one more responsibility or job, you could say something like, "I'd really love to, but I am just not able to do that at this time."

Rather than trying to dissuade your guilt with gifts and wrong food, or trying to compensate by giving your children their way, find ways to rearrange your schedule to be able to spend more time with them. Rather than overcompensating because you waited so long for the child, or because the child's father left the home, or because the child suffers from sickness, find ways to help the child work through these difficulties in a biblical and disciplined way.

When that child is 17 or 18 years of age and has a troubled life, no one is going to care that he faced these difficulties as a young person. They won't want to hear you say, "The reason he's in so much trouble is because he was sick when he was little, and I couldn't spank him." Don't fall into that child-rearing trap which will cause you and your child to have to pay for the rest of your lives.

You waited a long time for the baby. When you took that baby home, you couldn't believe it. That baby was so precious. But that child is no more precious than the one who was given to parents soon after they married. However, you thought you wouldn't have a child, and so you have decided you are going to be very good to that baby. That's your little baby, the one you didn't even know if you were ever going to have. *Watch out, mother, watch out!* That little precious baby can turn into a witch at 15 or 16 years of age if you don't decide to love her enough to discipline and correct her when she is young.

In order that you can properly love, discipline, and train your children to be adequately prepared for adulthood, do not overcompensate for special, difficult, or unfortunate circumstances.

CHILD-REARING TRAP #6
Spanking Children Before Friends and Relatives

There are several reasons to never spank your children before other people, and the first is that you are risking the possibility of being reported to the authorities for child abuse. You can be turned in to the authorities even if you administer a proper, biblical spanking.

Secondly, those people may not turn you in to the authorities, but they will often feel free to give their opinions, and you don't need another opinion. If you need an opinion, it should come from someone to whom you have gone about child rearing. Counsel should come from an older or wiser person who has the biblical wisdom and knowledge to guide you.

Use resource people. I have a friend who has a little girl going on two, and that child is quite a go-getter. I gave that friend the names of two ladies who did a pretty good job of rearing girls with personalities much like her daughter's.

That friend of mine is talking with those ladies once or twice a month. When new things happen, she has reinforcement from people who have been where she is. We all need godly resource people—people who have really loved, cared for, and worked with the same type of child that we have.

What we don't need is every opinion of every friend and relative. Don't open yourself up to get opinions. Get opinions from your husband, and maybe one counselor such as a pastor or a godly woman in the church, but do not get opinions from your friends and relatives.

If people tend to give unwanted opinions, just respond with, "Uh...uh...yes... oh, yes that's interesting." But don't get involved in a big conversation about the opinion or argue about the opinion. Oftentimes we program our friends and relatives to give their opinions by correcting and disciplining our children in front of them, or even by stating our concerns about our children to them.

The third reason not to spank children in front of friends and relatives is that you want to protect the child's dignity. You certainly would not want to be corrected by your superior in front of your co-workers. The same holds true for your children. Protect their dignity by removing yourself and your child from the situation and finding a private place to administer the needed discipline.

CHILD-REARING TRAP #7
Viewing Spanking and Disciplining Your Child as an Interruption

Don't consider taking time for spanking as an interruption. I know that so often we mothers don't spank, don't spank well, or don't talk to the child well because we are in the midst of sewing a dress or some other project that has a deadline. Even if we are not on a deadline, it seems like an inconvenience to stop what we are doing and take the time to discipline or train our children.

Maybe you are baking a cake and if you don't get it out of the oven right now, it will burn. Let me tell you, just go ahead and let the cake burn. A burned cake is not too much of a tragedy, but a ruined child will hurt you the rest of your life. You'll never remember you burned the cake; or if you do, you'll get some laughs from it. But you sure will remember that you spoiled the child. You will remember not just two days from now, but two years from now, twenty years from now, forty years from now, and for as long as you live.

It seems that too often cakes, dresses, telephone calls with our friends, and people at the door get more attention than our children. The time you take spanking that child can be quality time. People act as if quality time is doing fun things and having a good time with your child.

Quality time can be working together. It can be talking over serious problems together or having fun together. But it also can, and should be, quality time while you are disciplining that child.

Stop the project. Turn off the oven, sit down, take a deep breath, and do what needs to be done with your child. Pray and ask God, "Please help me to take every bit of time this child needs so that someday the child, the child's mate, and the child's children will not suffer. Let me never count this as an interruption, but rather a privilege that I have the opportunity of training my child."

When you are thinking this way, your child will sense the difference. Children know when they are an interruption, just as they know when they are not. Thinking this way will give your child the confidence to know that he is important to you—so important that you will leave anything you are doing to give that child what he needs.

If you will consider a spanking as quality time rather than an interruption, you won't be frustrated by the length of time it takes. This will involve your talking kindly and evenly, spanking, and talking again. There should be no anger, frustration, or edge in your voice if you are going to make the child feel he is not an interruption.

If, after the spanking, the child's spirit has been closed to you because he is angry, help the child get over his anger or the spanking has not been completed. After the spanking, the child should be able to tell you why he was spanked. He should talk respectfully and lovingly. Have a loving time at the end and a praying time where the child asks forgiveness. Be sure the child knows and feels that Mama loves him.

After this time of discipline is finished, go back to whatever you were doing. If there's not time to complete the project, maybe you won't put the whole sewing machine and everything away. Why don't you take a shortcut on that? Take a shortcut on supper. Take a shortcut on a cake. Take a shortcut on a dress. But don't take shortcuts on a spanking.

If you feel at a loss or feel you don't really know how to spank, study to find out. Listen to sermon tapes and read Christian books. Talk with people who have reared happy adult children. But don't let the disciplining of your children be an interruption!

CHILD-REARING TRAP #8
Using Too Many Babysitters and Not Giving Those Caregivers Instructions and the Authority to Use Those Instructions

I know it is not always easy to find a babysitter. Sometimes it seems that your schedule requires you to be gone more than normal, and your child has to be with a babysitter more than usual.

People, watch out. What's happening to some little children while being in the care of babysitters today should not happen to animals. And don't think just because the person you are leaving your children with is a relative that everything is okay.

Be extremely careful of allowing unsaved neighbors and teenagers to watch your children. I know there are times you feel you are between a rock and a hard place, but I've heard too many stories to not warn you.

I fear that we do more investigating of someone we have working for us in a job like cleaning our house, than we do investigating a babysitter. Of course, I know you can't go in and access the F.B.I. files on the person you are considering, but there are a lot of ways you can casually and nicely ask questions that will help you know as much as possible.

Try, right from the very start, to find two or three people to leave your children with and try to limit outside caregivers to those two or three people.

Give babysitters written instructions about your children—their eating and nap schedules, rules, what you want done about discipline, etc. It seems that we give more instructions to someone using our car than we do to caregivers of our children. You possibly won't even know where that car is two years from now, but you will know where that child is. Caregivers need to know what kind of discipline you expect and what kind of authority you are giving them. If you don't leave them with any authority, they are helpless to give the child back to you who is the same child you left. Children need consistency, and you must instruct the caregiver if your child is to have consistency.

When you return, ask the caregiver for a report about the children. Don't just ask, "Was everything okay? Here's your money," but really find out what happened in the children's lives while they were away from you.

Observe your children to see if they are acting strange in any way. Ask questions. I don't mean go around being suspicious and living in fear every second of your life. But we do need to be very cautious. I hate to discuss this because it's just sick. There are many great babysitters who are good with children, but you also know there are people who are not good with children and instead hurt the children.

You are so fortunate if you have a mother or sister or someone nearby whom you really feel you know. You are fortunate if you have someone you feel you can give instructions about the baby. But observe your children and know what is going on when they are under someone else's care.

Mothers do need time away from their children. Some of the best mothers I know get some time away from their children once in a while. I recall watching a young mother who spent so much time playing, singing, praying, teaching, loving, and working with her toddler that she came to a point where she just felt like she couldn't keep at it any longer and do the right thing. Her sisters took her baby for a couple of days while she went away with her husband and had a good time. She came back home refreshed and was able to get back in the groove of rearing a happy, contented, healthy, well-disciplined child.

I know that parents need to use babysitters. I just want to caution you to know your caregivers as well as possible, limit the number of caregivers you use as much as possible, and help your children get consistent, loving care from those who watch them.

CHILD-REARING TRAP #9
Letting Our Children Play with Other Boys and Girls Who Are Not Made to Obey

There is no way to completely prevent your children from being with other children who are not taught or made to obey. Just in the everyday happenings of life your children are going to be exposed to disobedient children—whether it be in Sunday school, at the grocery store, or in a Christian school.

I am not suggesting total isolation from everyone and everything to keep your children from being exposed to the disobedience of other children. What I am talking about is not letting your children play with and socialize with children who are not made to obey. Keep in mind the verse, *"Be not deceived: evil communications corrupt good manners."* (I Corinthians 15:33)

There are many cases where parents have good

standards and want the same thing you want—obedient children. But it's not a matter of wanting the same thing; ask yourself, do they make their children obey? Very few parents do. It seems that many parents who want obedient children don't know what to do or don't know how to teach their children obedience. Hopefully, the people with whom you associate want their children to obey; but the fact is, it really doesn't matter whether they want it or not if the children are not made to obey.

Know the children with whom your boys and girls play. Know their behavior, know their parents, and know as much as possible to determine if you want your children spending time with them.

Supervise your children in play with other children. I know a mother who is trying her best to teach her children to obey. Because she wants her son and daughter to have playmates, she invites children to her house where she can closely supervise the behavior as the children play together. She is able to guide the behavior more easily than if the other parents were present. She does, at times, have to stop the play and let the visiting children know that a certain type of behavior is not acceptable at their house. Because she is fun and corrects very kindly, it seems the guests are able to take the correction she gives and want to come back.

Attend parties to which your children are invited. Often young children are invited to birthday parties. I know of more than one mother who simply offered to help at the party (which is usually welcomed by the hostess) in order to be present. I also know that all of those mothers have been glad they went as they were able to learn if that was a home where they wanted their child to spend more time.

There will be some parties which you do not allow your children to attend because you know of the circumstances in that home. So often we feel called upon to "tell the whole truth and nothing but the truth" to everyone involved. You don't need to tell those parents—or anyone else—why your child cannot come to their house. Just make other plans and let the parents know your family has other commitments. In situations such as this, it is a good idea to send a gift even though your child will not be able to attend the party.

Use a babysitter when you are going to the home of someone whose children are not made to obey. You never want to say to a parent, "Now I can't come to your house because you have unruly kids, and I have good kids." Her kids might turn out just fine, and yours may not! Don't ever say what your kids are or aren't going to do. Neither do you want to just take your children and put them in a situation where they observe children for an entire afternoon who are not made to obey. As a rule, we become like those with whom we associate, and our children will more than likely return home with a disobedient attitude. So, if it is necessary to be with a mother who does not make her children obey and her children, use a babysitter to keep your children away from that situation.

CHILD-REARING TRAP #10
Believing It Is Too Late to Help Your Children

No matter what your age—whether you are in your forties or your eighties—if you have an adult child who is breaking your heart, don't let *anybody* tell you it's too late, no matter what the reason.

If you feel you did not train that adult properly as a child, you cannot change that. You have paid dearly, and your child will pay, but that does not mean that you can't do *something* now. It's not too late.

Do everything you can. I don't mean try to buy your adult children with money. I am saying to give them *time, attention, and love.* You may hate everything they do, but every time you want to just go cry into your pillow, do cry a little bit; but then get up and find something you can write them or do for them that you know they will accept and appreciate.

When a mother's heart is broken over her adult children, of course, she feels like crying all the time. But only God can take our negative feelings and opinions. Psalms 142:2 says, *"I poured out my complaint before him; I shewed before him my trouble."* Children need to see a joyful, victorious, contented mother who is trusting God while she is using every tool within her power to reach out to them with love and acceptance.

It may take years before they come to see you. Possibly when hurts come into their lives, they will ask you where you go for help. It may take time, but it's never too late to help your children. It may be too late to do some things for them, but I believe it is never too late to help your children.

You can make it your hobby to court your adult children to the Lord—*not* by sending tracts. Of course, if they did not grow up hearing the Gospel, be sure that you or someone else has talked with them about how to be saved. Once you have done that, it is usually not wise to continue sending tracts, Bibles, Bible verses, etc. What that adult child needs from you is love and acceptance.

More than one unhappy adult child has declared, "I don't want to hear any more of that Bible stuff. I'm not opening any more letters or packages from you. All you do is preach at me." You say, "What more can I do?" Let me give you some ideas.

Watch in the newspaper for little articles you think he might not have seen about his friends or people he knew in high school. This may even include people you didn't want him to be with as a teen. But if they were friends, what that says is, "Mom cares enough about me that she thought of me when she read that article and knew I would be interested."

Send funny cards that would remind the child of childhood days—ones that he would find humorous. Maybe you could write names under the characters or put little reminders of past happy times.

Take advantage of every holiday to send beautiful or fun cards. We never know what little acts of kindness can mean to our children. I believe that keeping in touch through sending cards at every holiday time gives them something to look forward to and lets them know you love them and are thinking of them.

Don't try to make points through your conversations, letters, or gifts. It is so tempting to want to get in our little points, but that simply says to our children that we are not accepting them for who they are right now. Acceptance is key if they are to feel home free. They know what you stand for without your making points with them.

Praise them and encourage them in every area possible. Possibly your son is drinking alcohol or is living with a woman to whom he is not married. Of course that hurts. But is he going to a respectable job faithfully? Praise him for his work ethic. Does he spend time with his children? Praise him for being a good father. People are dying to know they are "okay," and you can help your adult children know they are "okay" in your eyes!

It's never too late to give your love, your time, and your attention. God may take what seems like such a little bit and bless it just as He took the fish and loaves and blessed them.

CHILD-REARING TRAP #11
Mothering Your Child the Same at All Ages

You bring home that little baby boy and say, "Goo-goo!" But some parents are still doing it when that boy is a teenager. No wonder he pushes them away.

Realize as your child grows older that he is changing. A child is different from a baby. A junior higher is different from a child. A high-school teen is different from a junior higher. A college young person is different from a high-school child. And a child who is married is certainly different from an adult child living at home.

It is no wonder that many a daughter-in-law has difficulties with her mother-in-law. I hear wives telling how their mothers-in-law are seeing to it their sons still do certain things. They resentfully say, "My mother-in-law treats my husband like a baby."

What happens is that we don't move up in our mothering when the child moves up in his age. I realize that some mothers have five or six children, and maybe two distinct families in age. It does take somewhat of a juggling act as you are going to be mothering several different ways at the same time.

But I also know that God can help you do it. I believe in many cases that just being aware of the fact that mothering needs to change as the child grows will help many ladies.

———

I don't know what child-rearing traps the Devil is trying to use to discourage, distract, or defeat you with your own children or children with whom you work, but won't you join me in fighting these traps in order to help our young people to grow up and become happy, fulfilled, adults?

chapter fourteen

ℳre You Hard
of Listening?

*Andrew and Adam Beaman
with Dr. Jack Hyles*

"Lo, children are an heritage of the LORD: and the fruit of the womb is his reward." (Psalms 127:3)

Since children are an heritage of the Lord, we must give our children a godly heritage they can leave to their children and grandchildren.

Recently, when talking with some friends, we were deciding how to be seated at a restaurant in order to be on the "good ear" for two members of the group. The jokester at the table piped up with, "I'm not hard of hearing; I'm hard of listening." Those words jumped up on neon stilts to me as I thought how little any of us know about the art of listening.

Listening Might Be the Best Method of Preventive Child Discipline

We are pretty good with lectures, talks, and speeches—as we well should be—but I wonder whether or not some of those lectures could be saved or moderated if we were better listeners. There are times when children would tell us what they are thinking, what is bothering them about a group they are beginning to "hang out with," and then, even answer their own concerns if we were to carefully give them undivided attention accompanied by open ears, open eyes, and a closed mouth.

If a mom is really watching, she sometimes can hear what a child is not saying, know when to ask a non-threatening, short question, and go back to listening.

I'm afraid we want children to listen to us, but we don't want to listen to them.

Beware of Always Doing More Than One Thing at a Time

It's a lot of fun to do two, three, or more things at once. It is not always wise to do even one other thing when we are dealing with another human being. It's interesting to notice that Elaine Colsten, Music Coordinator at First Baptist Church of Hammond—who can play the organ, talk to the P.A. man or pianist on the phone at the organ, and answer a business question for one who approaches her while she's playing the organ at the church—takes time to stop, look, and listen when she comes upon a person while walking in a church or college building hallway. She can teach us how to do four things at once in the home and how to stop the world for one person.

What Teenage Girls Want Is Shocking to Me!

Probably I should already have known and not been shocked at the answers when I recently started asking teenage girls to tell me their favorite memory with their mother. Without their being programmed and almost without exception, the answers of approximately 150 girls in many different states of our country at several different times always ended with *time alone with Mom* as being their favorite memory.

Thinking at least a few girls would say their favorite times involved a big vacation trip, amusement park activity, or some other high-ticket item, I found my mouth falling open (in silence) as I heard one after another say:

"The time Dad and my little sister were gone, and Mom and I talked."

- "The time my mom and I went for a walk and talked."
- "The time Mom was in the hospital, and I got to be with her all of the time."
- "The time our car broke down, and Mom and I talked two hours while we waited for help."
- "The time Mom and I stayed up and talked after everyone else went to bed."
- "The time I was sick; Mom took off from work to stay with me."

Now, honestly, these are some girls, aren't they? Do you suppose when moms say, "You can never satisfy them. They want something more no matter what you get them," that they just don't understand? Could a girl be asking for a fourteenth purse (name brand at that) because she is afraid to ask for Mom's time? Does she even know she wants Mom's time? Is she afraid Mom will reject her if she just asks for time—no reason? Has the world been successful in making her think she no longer wants her mom?

When girls will be sick, go to the hospital, or be stalled in a car to have their moms alone and listening to them, they must be hungry for their moms.

Sometimes Working Together Is a Springboard

Recently one mother told me, "My daughter and I forged a friendship over the dishes. I didn't get a dishwasher as long as she was home."

This philosophy seems to go against watching about

giving undivided attention or doing two things at once. No, it may be that working together will provide the springboard for a girl to warm up to heart-to-heart talks as she can have her hands busy and her eyes averted. *The important thing is to remember doing the dishes isn't the goal in this instance.* It is a tool used to reach and teach the girl. If, at any time while doing a project together, the talk demands full attention, stop and give that full attention. Plan how to get back later to finish the job together.

At the W.M.S. South Pacific Circle meeting one month, Mrs. Mary Ruth Harrington, who has taught in the same Sunday school department for high school girls at First Baptist Church of Hammond for more than 50 years, told me a former Sunday school student was going to visit her that night. When I asked her what they were going to do, she said, "Nothing really." I can tell you without knowing that the nothing was something, or the high school senior would not have been there. I imagine Mary Ruth was not hard of listening that night.

Girls: Don't Use This Against Us!

I want to say a word to any young person who may be reading this book. We adults are so busy wanting for you, we are scared for you in today's world. It is very difficult to turn off the worries and just enjoy you. If we err, it's on the side of love for you. Give us time to try to learn to do better.

Let your moms know how much you enjoy their listening to you all of the times they do remember to do so—right on the spot tell them. Perhaps instead of your telling your mother she is terribly hard of listening, you could work at practicing being a better listener to her and others around you.

Moms, Memorize James 1:19

"Wherefore, my beloved brethren, let every man be swift to hear, slow to speak, slow to wrath." Do you think we are sometimes slow to hear and therefore swift to speak and swift to wrath?

chapter fifteen

Why Are We Losing Our Family and Friends?

Elijah Perryman

_____

"For I was my father's son, tender and only beloved in the sight of my mother." (Proverbs 4:3)

Find ways to cause your child to know he is yours and that he is loved.

_____

"And that from a child thou hast known the holy scriptures, which are able to make thee wise unto salvation through faith which is in Christ Jesus." (II Timothy 3:15)

Place Bibles around the house. Decorate with Scripture plaques and have Bible tapes playing part of the day.

It seems we can only stand by and listen as we talk to grandmothers who bemoan the fact that grandchildren seldom contact them in any way.

As we visit nursing homes, our hurt is compounded by the thought that the people talking could be us some day. They are telling the story of "No one ever comes to see me."

Anecdotes are being told about soul winners who have brought their converts into the church. They are dismayed and puzzled as to why one of these converts who was doing well in the work of the Lord all of a sudden disappears.

Many children are wanting to get away from home as soon as possible to sometimes seldom return.

Friends of a decade find someone with whom they are exclusive and never even call their old friends anymore. They say nothing is wrong, and as far as you know there isn't.

Spouses are leaving each other with absolutely no warning. "I had no idea our marriage was in trouble" is a cry so often heard. No one seems to have the answer.

Being known by my students for quoting and re-quoting a statement made by a Christian leader: "Behavior is always caused, and causes are always multiple," I certainly would never try to give one simple answer to this situation. It is too complex a problem for me to think I could handle the subject well. There is, though, one facet of the issue to which I've given much consideration. It is the question, "Why don't we praise people?'

So Why Don't We Praise People?

The Word of God says in Proverbs 27:2, *"Let another man praise thee, and not thine own mouth; a stranger, and not thine own lips."* This verse seems to indicate that God wants us to praise people, or He wouldn't tell us to let another man praise us. Doesn't that seem logical?

Proverbs 3:27 tells us to, *"Withhold not good from them to whom it is due, when it is in the power of thine hand to do it."* Most people thrill to a little word of praise more than they do to a tangible gift. A high percentage of people have found that they stay happier and more contented when they are giving honest praise!

If you believe giving praise is one answer to keeping people steady and not losing them, examine with me several reasons I have heard as ones given for not giving praise.

1. Fear of Taking Glory from the Lord

If you are a parent, you will know that you are doubly praised when someone praises your child. God is Creator of us all and wants to be the Father (the parent) of all mankind, *"...not willing that any should perish."* (II Peter 3:9b) People are His highest creation. Why wouldn't He want us to praise His creation? Certainly there is no good in man himself. Isaiah 64:6 says, *"But we are all as an unclean thing, and all our righteousnesses are as filthy rags; and we all do fade as a leaf; and our iniquities, like the wind, have taken us away."*

We can say, "Isn't that a beautiful tree? It gives us shade, houses, furniture, protection, and beauty," and no one thinks we're praising the tree too much. Why can't we praise people without people thinking we are worshiping man instead of God? We no more think man is God than we think trees are God just because we enjoy what they do well.

Could it be that we are neglecting our praising of God and therefore, feel guilty when praising people? Psalms 146-150 seems to show us that God wants praise. In fact, I don't believe He can get enough of it.

Praising God and all His creation, including people—who are His highest creation—would surely go a long way in taking care of our critical spirits.

I wonder if it would be too much out of context to take one of my favorite Scriptures, Matthew 25:40, which says, *"...Inasmuch as ye have done it unto one of the least of these my brethren, ye have done it unto me,"* to say surely when we throw a few crumbs of praise to a person, we are throwing them to the Lord?

2. Fear of Helping a Person Get a Big Head

"She talks about herself and the good she does all the time." Perhaps she wouldn't have a need to tell the good about herself if we were telling it to her. Do you *really* know anyone who has what some call the big head? Does a truly secure person have to act cocky? Then, what does that say to us?

When a person all but begs us for praise, we say, "I'm not going to give it because she asks for it." Why don't we give her what she needs before she begins asking? So often a person will say, "It's just the principle of the thing." What principle, pray tell me?! I'm afraid it is our *pride* rather than *principle* that keeps us from praising people and giving them what they need.

It seems that some Christians feel it is their mission in

life to help keep people from getting the big head. We need to remember that it is not our job to keep people humble. Critics, old age, heartaches, failures, and arthritis can care for that. Some of us act as if God put us on earth to keep people in their places. God can handle that if He wishes. It's not our job!

Have we not gone to the God of love, and His love letter—the Word of God—enough to get security? Being unable to give praise to others often shows a lack of security and confidence in God's love on our part. Is this lack in our own lives causing us to live out our feelings of, "I don't feel good enough about myself to say anything which makes another look good?"

3. Fear of Knowing How to Give the Proper Kind of Praise

Could it be that we don't know how to give praise because we haven't experienced getting it? Dwell on Psalm 139 and place your name where the pronouns are. Put yourself in the way of praise. Don't shun praise and good words as so many do because they don't know how to respond. When someone praises or compliments, you just smile and say, "Thank you." Then take that pearl of promise home with you to examine.

Determine to be what someone said you are even though you don't think you deserve the praise. Thank God for every part of it that is true. James 1:17 says, *"Every good gift and every perfect gift is from above, and cometh down from the Father of lights, with whom is no variableness, neither shadow of turning."*

4. Trading Praise

We don't want to praise anyone who doesn't praise us. There are people who don't particularly care for me, but that doesn't mean they are not good people. If I believe something good about them, I'm going to say it. When I've talked well about someone, I've had people tell me, "Don't you know they don't think much of you?" I may or may not know, but that has nothing to do with the fact that I think good about the person in some area. This business isn't a game of "tit for tat; you killed my dog; I'll kill your cat."

5. Fear of Giving Full Approval

We are afraid if we praise the person, he will think we condone everything about him. If you are a fundamental, Bible-believing, separated, soul-winning Christian, the person you praise will know your stand. They'll know what you don't like about that which they do.

Have you ever given your children or worker a compliment only to have them "blow it" in the next hour? You say, "See, that just shows praise doesn't help. I can't say a good word again!" No, praising good reinforces good. The child or worker falls all the time as she is developing, but we just notice it more right after we've exerted ourselves to praise her.

We want to hear our kids say good things about each other, but far too often, we won't praise them ourselves. According to Proverbs 31:28, the Proverbs 31 woman received praise, *"Her children arise up, and call her blessed."* Evidently, praise is something we ought to desire.

Is It Possible We Don't Realize the Importance of Praise?

If you don't realize the importance of praise, ask yourself, "To whom do people throng?" They go to those who give them a good feeling about themselves even if it is as false as rock star jargon.

Where does a man or woman go when he or she leaves a spouse for someone? Isn't it to a person who praises? "She (or he) understands me." What do they understand about them? They understand their need for praise, don't they?

Jim Jones seemingly was able to take scores of people away from their friends and family to death because he made them feel good about themselves.

We're losing church members because we do not give them a job, and neither do we help them develop a feeling of achievement.

While we're saying, "You'll spoil them," when parents are showing and talking love to their children, the world is captivating them with praise. The Bible says we will spoil them if we spare the rod. We're to drive foolishness from them by not giving them their own way all the time. But just as much as a child needs discipline and correction, that child needs praise and love and acceptance.

Go ahead and tell children how much you love them, what they mean to you, and how you admire certain characteristics in them. Kids are extremely vulnerable to any person who will show them a bit of love. The reason why is because so many people withhold the good that it is within their power to give. I think it is so sad to watch a husband or a child fall victim to someone who flatters. What that person really wants is their loved ones giving real, sincere praise.

Do We Really Mean It?

We want to be absolutely sure the person deserves praise, and we also want to be absolutely sure that we really mean every word we say. It is interesting that we want to be so sure praise is deserved but then don't seem to mind throwing out criticism at a drop of a hat. We usually don't worry about whether or not a person deserves our criticism.

Surely there's something about which we can truly praise almost anyone. Think on, pray for, and really dwell on the person; look for the good.

Will Praise Be Accepted?

Sometimes we are fearful about giving praise because we don't know how it will be accepted. If the receiver of praise hurriedly says, "Oh, no, give the glory to the Lord," we feel unspiritual and reprimanded.

Yes, a statement like that can make you feel a little uncomfortable, but revel in the fact that you are obeying a Bible principle and simply pray that the person will learn to accept compliments and praise in a way that will make others more comfortable. Surely God wants us to give a little praise to encourage people—His greatest creation—no matter what their response.

It is also good to keep in mind that no matter how a person responds to our praise, we never know the real impact of our good words. Your teenager may simply use the "Neanderthal grunt" (as Dr. Tom Vogel so aptly put it in his book, *May I Suggest...*) when you say something good about him, but he may come back years later and tell you how those words encouraged him when he needed it most.

Rather than basing our behavior on others' responses, it is wisest to act on the principles of the Word of God. We are not responsible for the actions and responses of others, but we are accountable for our own actions and words.

Who Cares What I Think Anyway?

Most people are so hungry for a bit of encouragement they would gladly take it from anyone—even Frankenstein!

Have you ever noticed how quickly a person has time to listen to you when you find a way he can accept praise? Possibly you'll have to come in the back door with it by asking him about how he learned something he knows, but it is imperative that you find the key to praise.

Let's quit losing our spouses, children, church members, Christian school students, friends, Sunday school class members, bus kids, and anyone else for the reason of a lack of praise.

You might want to keep a notebook of praises to God. When one little page is something about a person, send the person a copy of what you said to God about him. God, you, and the receiver will all be blessed. Don't say what you don't believe. But what little good you do believe about someone, give as soon as possible!

It seems as if the whole world is standing with outstretched, begging hands and pleading eyes that say, "Do you like me?" "Am I okay?" "Have I done anything good today?"

The woman in the line-up of wheelchairs in the nursing

home—the one who grabs your hand and tries to keep you—is so desperate she doesn't care about letting you know what most other people are trying to hide—a need of approval. Fill that need a little bit, and you might get in to show them how God can fill that cup of need to overflowing.

Think about it. Are we losing because we are not praising?

chapter sixteen

You Can't Tell My Folks I'm Not Theirs!

Julia Marlene
Schearer

Abigail Marlene
Keene

"Praise ye the LORD: for it is good to sing praises unto our God; for it is pleasant, and praise is comely." (Psalms 147:1)

Let's daily, hourly praise the Lord for He deserves it of us. Constant praise will buoy our own and our children's mental, physical, and emotional health.

"Behold, the third time I am ready to come to you... for I seek not your's, but you: for the children ought not to lay up for the parents, but the parents for the children." (II Corinthians 12:14)

Lay by what you can (in any way) for your children.

I was speaking at a ladies' conference when the youth pastor of the host church, who was taken into a home when he was 12 years old, made some startling statements in my presence. As I recall, his parents did not get to legally adopt him until he was with them several years. At the time I talked with him, he was married to a lovely Christian girl and was serving as an extremely successful youth pastor. The couple also had a beautiful baby girl. His words to me were, "You can't tell Mom and Dad I'm not theirs—no way. Every day I lived with them they told me they loved me no matter how I responded or reacted."

Boy, did my ears pick up! Most of you know my husband and I adopted a baby girl in 1962 and a baby boy two years later.

Some of you have written *Christian Womanhood* asking me questions about adoption. One of the questions you've asked came back to my mind as I listened to this youth pastor.

Sometimes I am asked, "Do you feel about adopted children in the same way you would about your own?" I can't answer that question because I've never had children by natural birth.

I can say the following:

• If I loved my kids any more than I do, it could be a sin as in putting them above the Lord.

• When my kids are hurting, there's a cloud that I have to fight constantly until they're not hurting so badly.

• When my kids are happy and feeling the taste of victory, I feel happier than when I am feeling a taste of victory for my own self.

• I forget they're adopted until others remind me.

• When I catch a glimpse of my kids out away from home, my ol' heart skips a beat.

I doubt I love my kids as I would if they were natural-born children. I think I love them more than if they were my natural-born children. We had to decide we wanted those kids enough to go to the adoption agency and let them question us, look at our records, and inspect our duplex until their hearts were content.

We wanted our children so much we accepted them the minute we saw them even though we were allowed to take time to think about it. We had prayed God would lead the case workers involved to present to us **our** children, and they are **ours**. Whether they are winning or losing, down or up, they are our children forever and ever.

If all this sounds somewhat like you who have children by natural birth, then you have the answer to "Do you love them as natural-born children?"

Perhaps there is a different feeling. I don't know. Maybe one loves natural-born children for different reasons from those adoptive parents feel. I know one thing. Until you've gone to an adoption agency and walked out with "your child" wondering if you should have paid a million dollars, you don't know that feeling.

Do you suppose God just takes care of it all so it evens out in His time, plan, purpose, and will? I think so!

The Bill Davis family

chapter seventeen

Stress Busters
for Mothers

*Marlene Evans with Sheila Short
and her daughter Jennifer*

———

"Rejoice with them that do rejoice, and weep with them that weep." (Romans 12:15)

Whenever possible, wash the dishes or load the dishwasher with your child. This is a great time to listen to the joys and sorrows of the day.

Mothers may think I am for escaping reality and not facing one's problems when they read my de-stressors. I definitely am not; I do feel we sometimes (when it is at all possible) need to put ourselves in a holding pattern for a short time.

I believe many relationships would benefit from applying some of the following principles and ideas listed in order to return to people and work projects refreshed. However, I believe that it is often our children who receive the brunt of our sharp words when we are under stress.

Dr. Don Boyd, principal of Hammond Baptist High School, says that from his observations in working with young people for over 25 years that it sometimes seems the worst abuse a child can receive is verbal abuse. So, the next time you are feeling frustrated and under stress, try putting some of the following ideas into practice.

- Divert to a positive immediately after dealing with a negative about which you can do nothing.

- Refuse to pray when your prayer time is worry with "Dear Lord" in front of it.

- Turn off the phone. One short call can easily destroy a fragile time of peace.

- Go away (for a time) from stressful situations in which you find yourself.

- Go toward people around whom you feel calm.

- Go to places that make you feel calm.

- Put work out of sight if at all possible.

- Memorize certain favorite calming passages of Scripture.
- Read Psalms until you feel yourself cool down.
- Know the music you need to calm you and use it.
- Concentrate on pleasing God when you feel you can't please anyone around you.
- Check the mail *after* you have regained your composure.
- Control e-mail, answering machines, and other electronic equipment in order to keep a peaceful living area.
- Leave the cordless phone out of the bathroom when taking what is supposed to be a relaxing bath.
- Don't give out a cell phone number and then go for what is intended to be a relaxing drive. When you are all wired up, you may get "wired."
- Doing more than one thing at a time can be exciting when you are working with things. Doing more than one thing at a time when you are supposed to be listening to or enjoying people can be stressful and usually keeps you from having successful relationships.
- Don't ask questions which lead to discussion of problems about which you can do nothing.
- Write down problems that come to mind when you are weakened by tiredness or illness so you will remember to handle them later.
- Exercise in a way you enjoy exercising.
- Realize good and exciting projects are also stressful and might need to be moderated.
- Make a cushion of time. If you think an errand will take one hour, allow one and one-half hours.

Even Jesus had times when He desired to be alone. *"And when he had sent the multitudes away, he went up into a mountain apart to pray: and when the evening was come, he was there alone."* (Matthew 14:23)

Jesus advised His disciples to get alone and take time for themselves. *"And he said unto them, Come ye yourselves apart into a desert place, and rest a while; for there were many coming and going, and they had no leisure so much as to eat. And they departed into a desert place by ship privately."* (Mark 6:31-32)

I kind of think Jesus would want you and me to have some time alone, don't you?

chapter eighteen

$\mathscr{S}$end Yourself
to Your Room

The Stagnaro children

"Be of the same mind one toward another. Mind not high things, but condescend to men of low estate. Be not wise in your own conceits." (Romans 12:16)

In restaurants, look for a round table when you have more than four so that no one feels out of the range of being seen and heard.

During the 1996 *Christian Womanhood* Spectacular at the First Baptist Church of Hammond, Indiana, Mrs. Judi Vest mentioned sending herself to her room at times when she had been in the midst of parent-child problems. That little idea has never left me since I heard her just briefly refer to it.

There are many occasions when sending ourselves to our rooms would help a great deal more than sending the children with whom we are dealing to their rooms. There are times when we need to retire to our rooms to get refreshment for ourselves. I can remember times when I lived all day long with children in a classroom or in my home, and I felt as if the kids were going berserk. Often I actually was the very one who couldn't see straight because of having an ache or a pain or being tired.

Of course, I could not go to my room when I was in the middle of a class day, but I could have asked the principal for a 15-minute replacement while I took stock of my needs. Perhaps I could have run to the corner drugstore for an aspirin or sat down with my feet up for a few minutes in a teachers' lounge or storeroom. That would have been the same idea as sending myself to my room.

Naturally, I was not able to send myself to my room when my own children were arguing as we crossed the street in the middle of traffic. However, I could have calmed myself long enough to deal wisely with my children as I made plans to head for home as soon as we crossed the street instead of continuing on until the bitter end of the shopping marathon. If I had it to do over again, I would hope I would send myself to my room instead of sending the children to their rooms during most hassles.

In trying to be a martyr by pushing on through a headache, a low-blood sugar time from not eating right, post-surgery weakness, or times of little or no sleep, we really open ourselves to doing and saying things that neither we nor the children forget very easily.

About 40 years ago, I pushed myself to the limit because I did not want to ask for help with an eighth grade class. I marched up to a relatively innocent boy to shake him as hard as I could by his shoulders. The Devil brings that scene back to me every once in a while even though God has forgiven me. I believe most of us could get relief before we go "up the wall" if we weren't too proud. I'm sorry to say that I believe most of us would rather hurt a child unnecessarily than hurt our own pride by going for help in order to get a much-needed temporary reprieve.

I am not advocating escapism, unless you call "escapism" leaving a scene temporarily in order to return permanently. In a lot of cases, we would not have to ask for help but just tell the children that we are going to our rooms to rest. Though we cannot enlist the help of a baby, keep in mind that infants can be easily made secure, if not content, for a short while.

What Should We Do in Our Room?

Depending on our own individual situations, we should do all of the following:

(1) Plan, (2) Pray, and (3) Pamper

The order in which these words are used should be determined by our needs.

If you have been fighting the flu for ten days and have finally "just had it," I doubt you can pray without just putting "Dear God" in front of a worry list that will only send you into depression, a crying jag, or possibly tantrums.

Perhaps we should sometimes pamper ourselves first. Pampering could include one or a combination of any of the following:

• Make a phone call to someone with whom you have wanted to talk without mentioning your present trauma.

• Shoot darts at your kids' pictures. (Just kidding!)

• Lie down with a wet cloth over your aching head.

• Take Tylenol® Sinus Allergy for your headache that is responding to no other medication.

• Eat a piece of delicious fruit you brought to the room from your kitchen stash. Eat it slowly, thinking about every bite as you enjoy it.

• If you are a scribbler, write out your feelings.

• Read a short article from some good magazine— perhaps *Christian Womanhood*—preferably not one on child rearing. Read a few soothing Psalms.

• Do some deep breathing exercises. (From what I am reading, this activity may be one of the best things you can do for yourself.)

• Listen to a couple of favorite songs.

• Lie down to rest whether or not you think you can sleep. Sometimes you wake up yourself with snoring and feel refueled after a relaxing ten-minute nap.

• Work at a crossword puzzle, a craft project, or just

anything that will cause you to focus on something other than your frustration.

Now, maybe it is time for prayer, or perhaps you poured your complaint out to God as soon as you got to your room. If you prayed in a way that gave you relief from your burdens, you can now thank God for your children and beg for His guidance as you plan.

Privacy in your own room gives a wonderful opportunity to plan for the good of your children. So often we go at children without a thought to a good plan of action. As we plan, we need to be wise as serpents and harmless as doves. *"Behold, I send you forth as sheep in the midst of wolves: be ye therefore wise as serpents, and harmless as doves."* (Matthew 10:16)

Let's send ourselves to our rooms for a happier, more enjoyable time in working with children.

In summary,

• Sometimes send yourself to your room rather than sending the children to their rooms when trouble is brewing. In the privacy of your room, pamper yourself in a way that will refresh you to return to the scene of action.

• Pray in your room, thanking God for children and begging for His guidance in dealing with them.

• Plan a course of action for dealing with the challenges of working with children.

P.S. You may want to review Judi's article entitled "Go to Your Room!" on page 8 of the March 1997 issue of *Christian Womanhood.*

The Corey Seulean family

chapter nineteen

$\mathscr{L}$ighten Up!

*Ashley, Trent, Trevor,
and Trey Cowling*

"Honour thy father and mother; which is the first commandment with promise; That it may be well with thee, and thou mayest live long on the earth." (Ephesians 6:2, 3)

Helping children to learn to honor their fathers and mothers is giving them the possibility of things going well with them.

One time when my children and grandchildren were visiting from Papua New Guinea, I was still very, very sick with chemotherapy. And so, the children had to just stay away from me and were told, "Don't go around Grandma. Grandma is sick." It seemed to me that my condition was forcing them to have memories of a very "un-fun" grandmother.

Months later I was starting to feel better and was scheduled to speak at a Hyles-Anderson College graduate's church for a ladies' conference. Pastor Dan Kaighen in Connecticut said, as he saw I was so much better, "While you are feeling better, shouldn't you go to see your daughter and her family in New Guinea?" That church took up $730 to start a fund in case we could go at Christmastime. They said we couldn't use it for anything else. We were able to take that trip, and my husband and I were able to make some fun memories with our children and grandchildren.

One of the major reasons I wanted to make that trip was that I wanted for my kids to remember me as a fun grandma. I don't believe very many fun mothers or grandmothers exist. Far too many of us make comments such as, "I can't stand the noise," or "I'm busy right now," or a number of other foolish statements, and that's how our children remember us.

Unless you are sick as unto death, find a way to stand that noise. Maybe you could stuff cotton in your ears. If you are busy, be busy at times when the kids and grandkids aren't around. Whatever it takes, find a way to have fun with the children in your life.

One of the reasons I believe there are not very many fun grandmas or mothers is that we are so scared. I understand why. There are so many temptations. There are so many possibilities and ways to do wrong.

Therefore, we are constantly saying, "No, no, no!" But no one wants to be remembered that way. We want to be remembered as fun people. Why not say, "Hey, I've got an idea."

My niece said something during my recovery from one of my chemotherapy regimens that just thrilled me to death. I felt with my having been sick that I had not been much fun. When I said to her, "I've got an idea," she responded with, "Aunt Marlene, when you have an idea, it's exciting!"

Oh boy, did her words mean a lot to me. Do you ever have an idea? Even if you don't think you have an idea, excitedly say those words while you are deciding real fast on an idea. You can do it with a little balloon or little blow bubbles. You can do it with a little ball or do it with a little piece of wax paper. There is a way to have some fun. Lighten up, folks, and try to figure out some fun things to do with the children in your life.

If you don't, the kids will have to go someplace else to ever have fun. You might think, "Well, my kids would never..." Don't count on it. Most kids want fun badly enough that if they don't find it in the right places with the right people, they will go to the wrong places and the wrong people to find it.

If you have a close relationship with your children—your children of any age—you are extremely rare. We must find some way to develop closeness with our children. The more I watch families who are close, the more I am convinced that one of the big factors is the family having fun together.

It is sad that when I see a mother and daughter who are close, it stands out to me. How terrible it is that close parent-child relationships are rare—even in our fundamental Christian circles.

Find a Way to Say "Yes!" Instead of "No!"

Sadly, we are finding our young people deciding they don't want the Christian lifestyle. Too often, it is a situation where there have been too many "nos" without plenty of "yeses."

I don't believe young people mind the "nos" if we are giving about ten "yeses" to every "no." Kids want to have fun!

One time I was in Mesquite, Texas, and met the parents of one of our Hyles-Anderson College girls. The parents told about how their family always visited large fundamental churches to hear hard preaching during vacation. They also told how the children listened to preaching tapes when they went to bed at night. The children seemed to love hard preaching, and though they've moved away from home, they still love it!

I said, "How? What did you do?"

The parents said, "We've always done lots of things the kids wanted to do along with the preaching. The kids who didn't get the preaching didn't get the fun our kids got."

If children are going to have a lot of hard preaching and a lot of "nos," they need an awful lot more of their kind of fun.

You're Not Fun?

Maybe you don't feel you are a fun person. One day, I had an interesting conversation along this line with Belinda Casteel, Dean of Women at Hyles-Anderson College. She said, "I am not a fun person. Therefore, when I am going to be with young people, I always take a fun person with me. They make the fun happen, and I am the *encourager* of the fun."

I had never thought of Belinda Casteel as not being a fun person, but that day I realized the reason. Because she wants the young people at Hyles-Anderson College and the teenagers in her Sunday school classes, and the ladies in the music groups she directs to have fun and because she does bring someone in to make that fun happen, people think of her as a fun person.

Belinda went on to explain to me that she sees several stages of being known as a fun person. The first type is the person who resists and puts down fun. They discourage fun and put it down as a waste of time. The second type is not fun herself but encourages fun in others. Lastly, the third type is the instigator of fun.

She said that she had started in the first group, and just wanted to get work done without wasting time having fun. She has moved into the group who encourages fun, and I believe that I now see her even instigating the fun.

In my book, *Comfort for Hurting Hearts*, I wrote a chapter entitled "Jesus, Our Fun." I listed step-by-step points in that chapter about how to learn to be a fun person if you do not feel you are one. Sometimes, people who were fun in their youth have lost their fun because of heartbreaks, illness, and responsibilities. If you struggle to be a fun person, I would encourage you to get that book, study that chapter, and begin little by little adding fun to your life.

Your being a fun person or a person who encourages fun will increase your opportunities of having eternal influence on young people. Just ask a young person who her favorite teacher is. Then ask why. The answer is usually, "He is so much *fun!*"

Now, fun isn't just all giggles, and parties, and hoopla. Fun can also be simple things such as lying on the deck together at night, looking at the stars. Fun can be looking at the clouds on a summer day and naming the objects you see.

I once read a tremendous story of a man whom I presume was probably not a Christian. He was telling about why he wasn't, as a writer, doing all that he could do to get ahead in his chosen profession. He talked about how he and his wife had adopted a child and how much time he was giving to this child. I want to share portions of this article with you.

> *Still later Tommy and I lie in bed together— the father and son, watching a television documentary about the Battle of Britain. Tommy asked me dozens of questions, most of which I could barely answer. Then without a word he lays his head on my chest. After ten minutes he says, "I'm tired Daddy," and falls asleep breathing lightly on my pajamas. It's like being in heaven... Only the place is here and now.*

The next day I show him the route I used to take across Flengo Creek on a foot bridge. "I got into a fistfight with a boy here," I say.

"Bet you killed him, huh Daddy?" Tommy replied.

"The only one on earth who thinks I could. I tell myself."

A close friend spoke about fathers who are too obsessed with their careers to spend time with their children. This is not just bad for the kids but also a waster for the parents. Children are a bottomless well of love and esteem for their parents if parents use only a little effort to tap it. While we are out trying to find love and esteem, we have a bottomless well of love and esteem we could be getting from our children. To the rest of the world, you are just a worker. To your kids, you could be an idol. For me who suffered constant humiliation in my work, this much philosophy had great appeal. This makes me envious at times about people who get...a lot more money. But never more than a few seconds. I feel I've learned what others have missed. If you're a hardworking American, you can usually make enough money to put bread on the table and keep a roof over your head. If you don't get promoted this month, there's always another chance. But the few years between five and fifteen when your child is articulate, insightful, and boundlessly affectionate will never come again. These years go by astonishingly fast. No billionaire can turn his sixteen year old into a *devoted, hold-your-hand youngster. No corporate title can replace the times when your son leans his head on your chest and falls asleep. No limo or private jet makes up for being there when your son is growing from a child into a young man. Time spent with Tommy isn't a distraction from the main event. It is the main event.*

Ladies, if we make our children the main event, we might have fun with them. And if we have fun with them, we very possibly will be close to them.

Lighten up!

chapter twenty

ℳake Your Home the Most Fun Place in the World

Marlene Evans with Stacey Lewis (l)
and Chaunah Macewicz

"Where there is no vision, the people perish: but he that keepeth the law, happy is he." (Proverbs 29:18)

We need to make the first move in taking the initiative to have a vision for our children.

In choosing our theme for the 2001 *Christian Womanhood* Spectacular, we decided on "It's a Party." I am terribly burdened about our need for fun. I feel as if most of us are so serious that we look like we've been out selling vinegar receipts or that we were weaned on dill pickles!

It seems as if we are just so down in the mouth. Our child rearing is not being done with fun. Our marriages are not being worked out with fun. Our church work is not being executed with fun. There's just not much fun.

Not only are most people not being fun, it is almost as if those people feel they need to be missionaries to those who do want some fun. Now, I don't mean it has to be a certain type of fun. I like certain types of fun that possibly you wouldn't enjoy at all. But, what is your type of fun? I think we are pretty stale people if we don't get some fun.

I guess I'm known as a party person. I do like to have parties, and I will admit that I want to turn everything I do into a party. I used to kind of feel badly about it and felt that I needed to defend that fact. Now I feel like I'd better teach it because I am seeing there is such a lack of fun in our homes, in our relationships, in our jobs, and in our churches.

I notice when a few of us go out and work together that when we start partying a little bit along with the work—add fun and laughter in with the work—better ideas come out, and the group seems more creative than when we are totally serious.

If there is any chance at all to make an occasion even a little bit festive, I do my best to make it happen. The other day I was with a group of people and someone said, "Well, now what are you celebrating?"

I answered, "We are celebrating just being here together." People, there is a lot to celebrate. As Christians on our way to Heaven knowing that Jesus will never leave us nor forsake us, we have a lot to celebrate every day of every year. It doesn't matter how serious things in life seem. It doesn't matter what illness has come our way or the way of a loved one; it doesn't matter what financial concerns or setbacks we might be experiencing; it doesn't matter what personal hurts we are trying to work through, we have a lot for which to be thankful and a lot for which to celebrate.

Just a few days before the 2000 *Christian Womanhood* Spectacular I was hospitalized because of my blood pressure and pulse rate. My pulse was going up to 200 if I even moved my hand or walked across the room. So, I was just sitting in my chair most of the time hoping not to have a heart attack.

Mayo Clinic in Rochester, Minnesota, is just six hours and fifteen minutes away from my house. That clinic has records of my case for 28 years. I was actually afraid to go any place, but since Mayo is so knowledgeable about my complicated physical condition, I called my doctor there and made plans to go directly to St. Mary's Hospital in Rochester. Two ladies who could spell each other off driving offered to take me. I got into the car wearing my robe. I didn't even want to chance changing clothes with my blood pressure and pulse going to such high numbers. We made only one stop—to use the restroom. I just put on a raincoat over my robe and rode in the wheel chair to the restroom!

We did arrive in just six hours and fifteen minutes. I was pushed into the emergency room by wheel chair still wearing my robe covered by a coat. I did not even put on my wig. (I was still bald from the effects of chemotherapy I had finished just weeks earlier.) I was in the hospital a few days and after a series of tests, they realized the problem was complications from chemotherapy. Because I didn't have the strength to do anything but lay in that hospital bed, I didn't have any makeup, my wig, or any jewelry on. I just had one of those hospital gowns on!

They gave me medicine, and after being very closely monitored for three days, my condition stabilized. (I was even watched by video 24 hours a day—what a way to look in the movies!)

By the time they took me off the monitor, I had the energy to put on my wig, jewelry, and some makeup. After doing so I walked down to the nurses' station. One of the ladies looked up and said, "Are you here for Marlene Evans?"

She had been in and out of my room all day and didn't recognize me. I said, "I am Marlene Evans." And I laughed. That whole ordeal was a very serious, life-threatening situation. But what does it help to not laugh? I got so tickled over her not recognizing me. What that nurse was saying is, "You looked terrible in there," and I knew it. She was so embarrassed, and I just laughed.

I really do believe that we can find humor in most situations if we will step back, take a deep breath, and look for the humor. It doesn't usually change the situation, but changing our attitude and our perspective to see the humorous side will help everyone involved.

How often have you heard an adult, especially someone who was reared during the Great Depression, say, "We were so poor, but I never knew it because we had so much fun at home." That is the key, ladies! Make your home so fun that the kids don't realize you are poor. Make your home so fun that the kids don't know you are sick. Make your home so fun that the kids don't know Grandpa is dying.

I said something recently that startled me. A friend of mine in Rochester, Minnesota, is a single gal. But I said to someone, "I never think of Chris Nelson as single." She has such a full life that I don't think "single." She is very involved in her church; she has junior-age girls to her house for slumber parties; she takes teenagers on weekend trips; she entertains adults in her home with lovely place settings and centerpieces; she watches out for the spirit of her co-workers at Mayo Clinic, and much more. Because she is such a happy, fulfilled person, I just don't think of her as single.

As I pondered this I thought, "That is the way it should be for all of us." If we are sick, people should not think of us as sick. If we are going through financial difficulties, no one should think of us as poor. What makes the difference is attitude, and our ability to have fun with the people in our lives.

I realize more than most that sickness takes its toll on a person's spirit. But find ways to be alone and get the rest you need so that when you are with people you can laugh and encourage their fun.

I realize that when one is about to lose a loved one in death, the hurt runs deep. But your children and your husband need you to be fun through that hurt. Go alone and cry so that you are able to go back to the people in your life with a smile and the strength to be fun with them.

Jane Grafton, my Special Assistant in *Christian Womanhood*, has told me of a very difficult situation in her family. I love what her mother did! Jane's grandparents were killed in a most tragic car accident just two weeks before Christmas in 1948. The newspaper account even told graphic details of the incident such as the fact that her grandmother was decapitated and the head was found lying in the middle of the road. They were a very close family, and Jane's dad, his two sisters, and their spouses were shaken to the core by this event.

Jane was not alive at the time, but her Aunt Lorraine has told her that none of the adults felt they could have Christmas that year. They just weren't in the mood. However, Jane's mother knew the need for things to be as normal as possible and the need for the children to have fun and offered to have Christmas at their house. Her Aunt Lorraine said that was so good for everyone. They were able to laugh again and have some normalcy, when things would never again be the way they had once been.

Now, I'm not saying to not face reality. I am saying that we need to make home the most fun place in the world as a refuge and respite from the difficulties and disappointments of life for our children and husbands.

Ladies, I don't know why you aren't having fun with your family. I don't know if you are sick, or if you are burdened with financial difficulties, or if you simply are so busy you don't see how you can find time to have fun. But let me urge you, if you want to be close to your family, you must have fun. As I mentioned in the chapter, "Lighten Up," you may not be the instigator of the fun, but you certainly can be the encourager! Find ways to be fun and laugh with your children!

The Matt Millen family

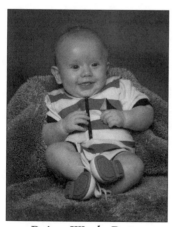

Brian Wade Bates

Troy Hill

chapter twenty-one

Please Don't Flunk Recess!

The Jeff Smale family

"Flee also youthful lusts: but follow righteousness, faith, charity, peace, with them that call on the Lord out of a pure heart." (II Timothy 2:22)

Teach your child that a strong person runs from places, people, and situations that could cause lustful thinking.

The other day I heard someone laughing about a person being so bad off that he flunked recess. Of course, this statement was given in a disparaging manner as if it would take some real skill to be stupid enough to flunk recess.

Personally, I think it takes more skill and ability to pass recess than to pass most any other subject in school. A student can earn high honors in all his school subjects but fail in life because he flunked recess.

The student who really gets reading, character building, and recess can probably learn anything else he ever wants to learn later on, but it's pretty difficult to go back to get recess. It's best to learn it all, but if choices have to be made, please don't choose to flunk recess.

It disturbs me when teachers act as if recess is only a "break time" for themselves. Some of the best lessons of the school day can be taught at recess.

The child who can enjoy a recess period without getting hurt or hurting others, either physically or emotionally, has achieved many of the skills needed for a good life.

He has probably learned or is learning to:

• Take turns	• Schedule time
• Share	• Organize
• Make decisions	• Blend
• Give up his way	• Lead
• Plan with others	• Listen to others
• Be flexible	• Follow

- Use teamwork
- Sportsmanship
- Exercise
- Play games
- Lose
- Win
- Pace himself
- Think fast
- Get along with people different from himself
- Have fun alone (if not chosen for a team)
- Constructively fill an unstructured time
- Make transitions easily
- Verbally communicate

Without these arts being developed, it is almost impossible to have a good marriage, to parent well, to be a loyal friend, or to be happy in your church or your work place.

Please, for goodness sake, don't flunk recess!

The Dave Hansen family

*The Bruce Alexander
family*

*Becky and Hannah
Alvey*

$\mathscr{I}$'m Tired of the Birthday Party Hassle

*Marlene Evans with Ruthy Grafton,
Carissa Grafton, Carly Wyatt, Jennifer
Rossman and Esther Pins*

"Speaking to yourselves in psalms and hymns and spiritual songs, singing and making melody in your heart to the Lord." (Ephesians 5:19)

Take a special ride during which you stop at any legitimate place the children want to stop as often as they want to stop since we so often say, "no time." Sing and laugh together.

I know mothers often dread thinking about providing another birthday party for their children. However, I don't think it has to be this way. Sometimes a child's birthday is at a very busy time of the year such as near, or even on, Christmas. Let me tell you about one party you could have—even in December.

Since it was Carissa Grafton's tenth birthday and she had never before had a birthday party with friends, her parents, Tom and Jane Grafton, had asked her to choose four friends to come to a birthday party at her home.

Jane picked up the girls—Carissa Grafton, Ruthy Grafton, Esther Pins, Jennifer Rossman, and Carley Wyatt—right after school and took them to a very nearby apartment where Carol Frye Tudor lived at the time. (Incidentally, I thought you might like to know that Carissa Marlene Grafton was named for **Carol** Tudor, **Kris** Grafton, and me—**Marlene**.)

Their second "happening" of the party was to stop by my house. By the time the girls got to my home, which is just a couple blocks away from Carol's place, they were full of chatter about their time with "Miss Frye." She had seated the girls around her parents' round oak table and had fed them a good and healthful after-school snack. She spent about a half hour letting them "experience" (to the fullest!) her grandfather clock, antique lamp, a girl and boy ceramic statue set, her kitchen Coke collection, and her dog Dusty. Carol also let the girls pound on the table and scream for a few minutes to let off steam after being in school all day.

After the girls spent a few minutes swinging happily on my double swing on the deck, my half hour with the girls found me presenting each of them a New Testament, writing their names, mine, and the date in each one and asking them what they liked about Carissa. They told me:

- "She isn't bossy."
- "She is willing to make things nice for us."
- "She gives up her way."

Her cousin, who is also her friend, Ruthy Grafton, said, "She's like a sister."

I told the girls about the call to me at 5:30 A.M. the day Carissa was born and how I acted when I found my name was part of hers.

All this time Jane stayed quietly in the background calmly enjoying her daughter's birthday party and taking pictures. I loved spending time with these young ladies. It was a treat for me, and they seemed to like it also.

Later I found that Dad (Tom Grafton) had pizza waiting when the girls got to Carissa's house. He also had a fire in the fireplace around which the girls sat to eat their pizza. Of course, everyone thought there would be a birthday cake. Instead, they were surprised with the ingredients for S'mores which were topped by candles. The girls sang, "Happy Birthday," as Carissa blew out her candles after which they prepared their own treat over the fire in the fireplace.

After gifts were opened, it was time to leave for church. Places to sit in the car and talk were organized for the trip to church. Mom had told the guests' mothers that she would take their daughters right to their choir room since their practice takes place just before Wednesday night Bible Study. This she did. She even waited for them to use the restroom at church so that she herself could escort them right to the choir director.

I seriously doubt that there were any hurt feelings among the girls, and I don't think there were any questions raised by the parents about anything that took place at the party.

Birthday parties probably are important, but they don't have to be huge, elaborate, or beyond what you can afford or can carefully supervise and control. In fact, there were no special decorations for this party, and it seemed that no one even noticed. With things such as a fire in the fireplace and pizza, the girls weren't thinking about decorations.

There's nothing wrong with a big bash sometimes if you can handle it in every way. Remember, though, that those big bashes probably won't provide the meaningful memories. Whether or not you have a birthday party or what kind of a birthday celebration you have should be dictated by your goals.

P.S. While preparing this chapter, I received a redbird postcard from Christy Baldwin and Melissa Harris, lovely teenagers from our church. Guess what? They chose my card while together on a sixteenth birthday trip to Shipshewana, Indiana! The honoree's mother, Mrs. Becky Harris, and three teens all went together. Of course, I'd be prejudiced toward a party that netted a card for me! Seriously, I think there is something very healthy about a 16 year old, who is celebrating her birthday, thinking about a 63-year-old woman.

chapter twenty-three

$\mathscr{T}$ake Your Toys
to Your Tots

*Marlene Evans, Doris Smith, Dianne Dowdey,
Chad Dowdey, and Amanda Evans*

"...and for seasons..." (Genesis 1:14)

Help your child prepare for the season coming up by studying seasonal pictures, preparing clothes for the next season, and watching the present season coming to an end.

People tell me that I often say, "Leave your world and enter theirs." Of course, I am trying to cause us to reach out to our spouses, our children, our other loved ones, our friends, and even to people we do not know. Since I have been known to talk out of both sides of my mouth, I will introduce a topic that seems to contradict the thought of leaving your world to enter the world of others. I believe, if you will follow closely, you will see that the two concepts can correlate.

I am now pleading with you to take your toys to your tots. Your toys might be crafting equipment, piano keys, cross country skis, gardening tools, a mechanic's tool box, a bicycle, a puzzle, a board game, or anything else you really like to do.

We have been taught so diligently by the world that we have our rights to our own fun that I am afraid we are not going to leave our world very long to enter the world of our children. When the child is very young, we often delight in watching his reaction to a mobile hanging over his head in the crib. We can't wait until we can report each new development that happens in the first few months and sometimes even in the first few years, but it gets old to us. About the sixth time in one day that a child wants us to go back into the sand box, read the same book, or go out to cautiously throw a ball back and forth, we have had it!

Is that attitude right? No, it isn't. We should have character enough to be patient and care enough about the child to enjoy and enjoy and enjoy his enjoyment.

So now, are we going to add a load of guilt on ourselves as well as a feeling of selfishness? The world has also taught us not to accept guilt. It's almost an unstated principle of worldly psychology that all guilt is bad. Thank the Lord if you feel guilty when you hurt another person. Be that as it may, you may turn from your child because of the conflict in your own life about leaving your world to enter theirs. Perhaps you do not have the character to deprive yourself of what you like to do for very long, whether it is work or play.

Let's just start wherever we are and build from there. Perhaps bringing children into your world of enjoyment will help you feel better later on about leaving your world to enter theirs. At least you will be with them in some world. Some of the "tots" to whom you will be taking your "toys" will not be such young children. They might be juniors through high school age, but they are young to you. What sport was your favorite as a child? Mine was bicycling. I could bike somewhat skillfully and cannot remember being able to do any other sport as well.

I foolishly gave up the sport in my early twenties. I cannot undo that. When I began to bemoan the fact, my husband, who is out riding with me every chance he gets, told me just to enjoy what I could do now. Now that I am back on a bike, I am trying to take my toy to any "tots" (younger people) in my life who will let me do so. That includes my younger sister, her husband, their daughter, their son-in-law, and their grandsons.

I have ridden with all five of my grandchildren. In each case, it took some doing, but it was worth it. Now that I am awake to the sport in which I can participate, I am out with the kids instead of sending them out to play without me. Instead of saying, "Grandma is too old and too arthritic," I am saying, "Let's ride!" They seem to like it a lot better; I know I do.

I recall one time when my two Evans' grandchildren and their mama Cathe were visiting. My sister Doris went all around her neighborhood borrowing appropriate bicycles for the three Tennessee kiddos—even to the corralling of a pair of training wheels. Then, Doris, Jerry, Chip, Dianne, 10-month-old Chad in a safety seat behind his mom, Cathe, Tony, Amanda, and I all took off carefully for a ride. We visited a beautiful cemetery which is located close to the relatives' houses, is safe, and has nicely paved roads. I keep my bike rack on the back of the car a lot of the time so that I can include my bike in my plans.

When we were visiting our children in Papua New Guinea, 10-year-old grandson Jordan gave up his adult-sized bike for me, but it was still hard for me to adjust to it because it is a man's bike. Jordan rode an extra child's bike they had. Grant (8) and Lindsay (5) had their appropriate bikes.

Grandpa and Grandma Ryder had sent money to make it possible for Jeff and Joy to get the kids bikes, and they had purchased the best they could get over there at a seaport town, Lei. I had to push my bike up a mountain trail that I was too unskilled to handle to get to the "smooth" airstrip where I could bike with the Ryder grandchildren. I didn't say that taking your toys to your tots would be easy. I do say it is worth it.

If your toy is the piano or some kind of music,

introduce children to music even if it is through a little toy flutophone or some rhythm instruments. Let them enjoy music at their own stage right along with you. Don't always adjust to them but don't insist they adjust to you in the way and length of time they enjoy music. Let them just catch your enjoyment of it. Don't start them in piano lessons at two years of age. Don't insist on two-hours-a-day practice at five years of age. Just enjoy your music and your children together.

I watched my son-in-law teaching football to his two young sons while I was in Papua New Guinea. Now, I know for a fact he loves football—especially his hometown team the Pittsburgh Steelers. The boys had on Steeler uniforms, and they were learning fundamentals of the game—but all at their interest, age, and attention level—not at Jeff's.

Three of my favorite hobbies are reading, writing, and checking out pretty birds. I'm sure my kids could have not escaped my obvious delight in those things, but I never noticed them taking an interest in them particularly until they reached their thirties. David has his own bird feeders to which he is very attentive, and Joy is quite a writer as she describes her missionary experiences.

Introduce Them to Your Kind of Play!

When children, preteens, and teenagers are approached with "toys," their immediate reaction might be coolness because they don't know how to be warm. Don't react to the coolness. Instead ask yourself some pertinent questions:

- Have I shown them how to care about people?
- Have they seen how to care about people?
- Do they have to become cool, just because they

don't know what to do?

Just as it can be difficult for us to leave our world and enter theirs, it will be difficult for them to leave their world and enter ours. But sometimes I wonder if we are not missing it with our children because we don't take our type of play to them.

A lot of times adults never get to play because we always play what the child wants to play. Don't we want to bring them into our kind of play? What do you like to do? What did you like to do when you were a kid? Can you remember when you did anything you liked to do?

I know a lot of you say, "If I could just have a whole day to lie in bed and read...." That is not the kind of activity about which I am talking. Neither is talking to another woman, without interruption, for four hours. Those two happenings are not what I am thinking. I realize many feel those are the biggest needs of every woman.

Other than reading and having a heart-to-heart chat with a close friend, what did you like to do when you were a kid? Are you sure you can't be doing it now? Why couldn't you be doing it now? Figure out a way that you can incorporate your kids into your kind of play.

It seems to me there ought to be three "yeses" for every "no" a person wants to get across to a child. If we need three "yeses" to every "no," we are going to have to spend a lot of time saying, "I've got an idea," "Let's do...," "Let's try...," and every other positive sentence which can be voiced. Whatever you do, do not give up your toys. Furthermore, take your toys to your tots.

- Decide what you like to do.
- Find a way to bring any children with whom you

associate into any appropriate activity.

• Allow children to enjoy your toys at their own age, interest, and attention level.

• Do not insist that your toys become their toys. Just introduce them to your interests.

The Dan Parton family

chapter twenty-four

Some Questions I've Been Asked and Some Thoughts I've Had Concerning Child Rearing

Anthony Evans

"A good name is rather to be chosen than great riches, and loving favour rather than silver and gold." (Proverbs 22:1)

Make much over your child's full name (i.e., John Allan Jones). It is important for him to know he is the only one who can make and keep his name a good name.

The following is a series of questions I have had the privilege of addressing in meetings, answering in letters, or perhaps in counseling sessions. I have found that counseling sessions are often a good indicator of what is happening in our homes.

How Can I Help Squelch Teenage Peer Pressure While My Child is Young?

Are we the guilty ones in teaching our children to live their lives by peer pressure? You ask, "Why, Mrs. Evans, what do you mean? I tell my teenagers not to go by their friends, but by Jesus, the Bible, their parents, their pastor, their Sunday school teachers, and other godly leaders."

Yes, but what did you and I say to our children when they misbehaved when they were young? We probably made statements or asked questions such as,

- "What will your friends think when you are crying and fussing like that?"
- "What would Susie say if I invited her into your room to see how you leave it so messy?"
- "Look at those kids over there. They are sitting there eating nicely looking at you acting so badly."
- "What do you think the kids in your class would think if they saw you sucking your thumb?"

Sound familiar? If these types of questions sound familiar, don't wonder why your kids as teenagers are particularly subject to that which is called peer pressure.

By the way, we older folks are sometimes pretty susceptible to so-called peer pressure ourselves. How many of us will still ruin our lives trying to please or seem "cool" to our peers?

Let me tell you that a good case of cancer like unto death can surely put you back into perspective. When you think you're on your deathbed, you are only caring whether or not you pleased Jesus during your lifetime. You suddenly don't give a hoot whether or not you pleased your peers.

Now back to the subject of rearing or teaching of children, grandchildren, students, or any child we have the opportunity to influence. Let's make statements such as:

- "Wonder what Jesus thinks..."
- "Do you want to please Jesus?"
- "You're making Jesus so happy when you obey."

Let's rear our children to please Jesus, not peers.

> *Jesus loves us when we're good,*
> *When we do the thing we should.*
> *Jesus loves us when we're bad*
> *Though it makes Him very sad.*

Let our prayer be and let us help the prayer of all the children we influence be, *"Let the words of my mouth, and the meditation of my heart, be acceptable in thy sight, O LORD, my strength, and my redeemer."* (Psalms 19:14) If our words and our thoughts are acceptable unto the Lord, we will be pleasing anyone God wants us to please. What else matters?

Blended Families

I have had mothers say to me, "I feel strange referring to my child's father as his real dad when my husband is doing most of the parenting I feel a real dad does. What should I say?"

I believe the best way to refer to a father who is not able, for one reason or another, to live with his child is as the "birth" father. No one can take that title from the birth father. Our daughter saw her birth father for the first time when she was 24 years old. He was in a wheelchair as a result of being shot by his third wife. No matter what else was or was not true about his life, he was still our daughter's birth father. (Joy just received word that he died several months ago.)

When a man, such as your husband, has walked real floors, paid real bills, and done real nurturing, I would think it would be difficult to hear someone else referred to as "the real dad." In fact, to further compound difficulties that are already rampant enough in these situations, the child will sometimes say, "You are not my real dad," when the on-site parent tries to discipline the child. Using correct terminology could spare feelings as well as create a better climate in the home.

———

Another question I have been asked is, "What advice would you give someone who has a broken home? My parents divorced while I was at college. How do I decide with whom to stay or how to divide time equally between the two? I'm hurting so much over this situation. How do I not show that hurt?"

———

I don't know that you can or should refrain from showing your hurt. You can keep yourself from utter despair by putting your mind on others' hurts, including those of your parents.

Three lines of reasoning that you, as a young adult, can use over and over which will help guide you are:

• "Mom (or Dad), I'm not qualified to counsel or make judgments. Have you thought about going to (a godly pastor)?"

• "Mom (or Dad), I'm going to be with (the other parent) on Tuesday all day. I can be with you on Wednesday or Thursday." (Let a man of God who is objective help you know how to divide your time.)

• "Please don't ask me to tell what is happening at the other parent's residence. I don't want to seem to be against either one of you. I need both of you, and I hope you both need me."

The consistent use of statements like these will help a child survive this very hurtful time in her life.

As we see more and more blended families, we see more and more difficulties in blending those families. If you are trying to work out the extenuating circumstances of a blended family, or if you are in the position of trying to help others in that situation, let me urge you to order a video or cassette tape by Dan and Janice Wolfe in which they address the subject of blended families in a most practical and helpful way. I believe they address every major issue facing blended families, and they give biblical answers that are giving hope and help to so many. The tape is available from *Christian Womanhood*, 8400 Burr Street, Crown Point, Indiana 46307.

"I just found out that my daddy is not my real daddy. I have mixed feelings about it. I wish I could get it straightened out in my mind. Can you help me?"

I'm going to share a copy of a letter I wrote to the daughter of a friend of mine. In this case the girl's natural daddy had been killed when she was very young.

Today your mother told me that she is going to tell you something which will be a shock to you. She felt so badly that she had not told you earlier. I know she wants the very best for you. She just wanted to shield you from anything she thought would hurt you. Your mother loves you very much. If she made a mistake in her timing of telling you about your dad, it is only because she loves you so much. Please let your mama know that you love her and appreciate her wanting to spare you anything that might trouble you. This is a hard thing for her. You will be showing that you are going to be a woman used of God if you care more for her in this situation than you do for your own feelings. Also, remember that the man you thought was your natural dad definitely is your real dad— not as the world thinks of "real," but as God thinks of "real." God has given you the love of a dad, and that is for real.

I can't help but hurt a little bit for you, because I just wish this world were perfect and that everyone had her own natural mother and father. Yet, I can't help but rejoice with you in that you have two parents who love you dearly. This will be one of your biggest tests of life. How you respond to it will determine what type of person you are. Start thanking God for everything He has given you instead of looking to what you have not had.

I want to do something special for you. I am doing this at this time in order to help you get your mind on something new. I am not trying to make up to you for anything I think has happened in your past. You understand that I want you to put your mind on something exciting, new, and different. Will you please take the enclosed money and buy a new outfit that will show you to be a feminine girl, a different girl, a girl used of God?

Proverbs 3:5 and 6 says, "Trust in the LORD with all thine heart; and lean not unto thine own understanding. In all thy ways acknowledge him, and he shall direct thy paths."

Control My Tongue

"All the good that I do with my children for weeks and even months is often undone in a moment of frustration with my thoughtless and often harsh words. How do I learn to control my tongue and my temper?"

1.   Saturate yourself with Scripture. Psalms 119:9, 11, "*Wherewithal shall a young man cleanse his way? by taking heed thereto according to thy word. Thy word have I hid in mine heart that I might not sin against thee.*"

Proverbs 16:32, "*He that is slow to anger is better than the mighty, and he that ruleth his spirit than he that taketh a city.*"

Proverbs 25:28, "*He that hath no rule over his own*

spirit is like a city that is broken down, and without walls."

2. Pray about this matter. *"Pray without ceasing."* (I Thessalonians 5:17) Pray about everything; worry about nothing.

3. Run from the scene of temptation until you can return to handle it rationally. If you cannot leave bodily, at least leave mentally.

4. In a difficult situation, start looking for things about which you can say, "Thank You, Lord."

Undesirable Behavior

"My baby bites. He bites me and other mothers on the leg. He also bites other children in the nursery. What should I do?"

In answer to this question, Mrs. John R. Rice said, "When the child bites someone, immediately he should be spanked. He will soon get the idea that it does not pay to bite people. When he bites, emphatically say, 'No,' and spank hard. Proverbs 22:15 says, *'Foolishness is bound in the heart of a child; but the rod of correction shall drive it far from him.'* Proverbs 29:15 says, *'The rod and reproof give wisdom: but a child left to himself bringeth his mother to shame.'* Proverbs 29:17 says, *'Correct thy son, and he shall give thee rest; yea, he shall give delight unto thy soul.'* "

Are You Listening to Me?

"How important is listening when it comes to child rearing?"

An 11-year-old girl recently said to her mother, "Can the other kids ride in the front seat, and you and I get in the back seat? I need my diary."

The mom said, "What do you mean, Honey?"

The girl answered, "I think of you as my diary, Mom."

How many kids would love to have you be their diary? You would be surprised how few have a listening ear cupped their way.

You say, "They don't come around me." Perhaps that is because you tell your own problems incessantly.

Be a kid's diary by keeping your mouth shut and your ears open.

The Tracy Ross family

Megan Kingsbury

Cara and Jacqueline Ranft

chapter twenty-five

Home for Thanksgiving

Amanda Evans

"And we know that all things work together for good to them that love God, to them who are the called according to his purpose." (Romans 8:28)

Be sure to point out to children those seemingly bad things that are obviously working out to the good already.

One Thanksgiving night, my family and I were sitting around Bud and Bertha Frye's round oak table. To the surprise of us all, their own son Keith came rushing into the house to say he was starved.

Bertha got up from the table, fixed a big plate of Thanksgiving Day leftovers, and heated it for Keith. After he ate enough to keep him alive, he started talking with us. I was particularly curious as to why he couldn't have had a Thanksgiving dinner someplace that day.

He explained it this way: "I was hauling oil out to one of the ships in the lake (Lake Michigan). The people on the ship asked me to eat with them. They had food of every kind from every port in the world, but I knew Mom would have leftovers. I waited to eat until I could get here."

This comment was truly something to think about. A man in his mid-20's with plenty of money in his pocket and a meal offered from exotic ports was willing to pull his 18-wheeler to the front of his parents' door to get Mom's leftovers!

"Better is a dinner of herbs where love is, than a stalled ox and hatred therewith." (Proverbs 15:17)

chapter twenty-six

Keep Your Eye
on the Ruby

Jaclyn and Brittany Staton

"But Jesus called them unto him, and said, Suffer little children to come unto me, and forbid them not: for of such is the kingdom of God." (Luke 18:16)

Take one of your children alone to a motel or a friend's house (who may be gone and will let you use her house) with a special project the child is working on and all materials needed to be his or her personal assistant in the project. Be like Jesus as He felt children were worthy of His time.

We never know what one little idea or statement can change a young person's life. Maybe this chapter will help you help your girls to stay pure for the marriage altar.

The little statement, "Keep Your Eye on the Ruby," was lifted straight from a letter I wrote to a teenage girl who had attended a *Christian Womanhood* Spectacular. She wrote, "Mrs. Evans, I dated a boy who was asking me for more of myself than I want to give. I was tempted, and then I heard your little talk about the ruby. I asked my parents for a ruby ring for Christmas or my birthday and decided I was going to use it to remind me to be pure. Whenever I am tempted to date a boy I know will try to get what I should not give, I look at my ring."

Now, many of us have let a redbird remind us of God's love for and to us. A rainbow was issued by God for a token of trust and love between us and God. *"I do set my bow in the cloud, and it shall be for a token of a covenant between me and the earth."* (Genesis 9:13) Likewise, a ruby—one of God's gifts in the earth—can be used to remind us to be what God wants us to be. Proverbs 31:10 says, *"Who can find a virtuous woman? for her price is far above rubies."*

A ruby is a precious stone, a red crystallized variety of corundum. It is red in hue, of high saturation and low brilliance. It is made of the hardest material of any gem except the diamond. Pure, transparent or translucent corundum is prized as a gem, called according to its color: sapphire (blue), ruby (red), and by other names.

I wrote the following in response to that teenage girl's letter to me.

"Honey, I'm talking to you who wrote me such a beautiful letter about asking for the ruby ring to remind you to stay away from anyone or anything that would steal your purity. I commend you. Keep your eye on that ruby (tiny or large is not the issue) as a piece of material given from God's earth through the love of your parents in having it refined and set for you.

"Let it remind you that '...*her (your) price is (can be) far above rubies.*' (Proverbs 31:10b)

"Always remember, '...*the price of wisdom is above rubies...*' (Job 28:18b), and '*For wisdom is better than rubies...*' (Proverbs 8:11a)

"All of God's nature, redbirds and rubies and rainbows, and many other of God's gifts—trees, bodies of water, flowers, birds, and animals—have all been placed here for our good one way or another. Let's use them for good and for God.

"'*For the invisible things of him from the creation of the world are clearly seen, being understood by the things that are made, even his eternal power and Godhead; so that they are without excuse.*' (Romans 1:20)

"'*But ask now the beasts, and they shall teach thee; and the fowls of the air, and they shall tell thee, Or speak to the earth, and it shall teach thee: and the fishes of the sea shall declare unto thee. Who knoweth not in all these that the hand of the LORD hath wrought this?*' (Job 12:7-9)

"'*The heavens declare the glory of God; and the firmament sheweth his handywork.*' (Psalms 19:1)

"Of course, we don't use a ruby as a talisman

(definition: a figure cut or engraved under certain superstitious observances of the heavens, supposed to act as a charm. Hence, something that produces extraordinary effects, especially in averting evil; an amulet; charm). The ruby cannot keep us from sin or make our price of much worth. Only the God Who made the redbird can give us love. The redbird is only a reminder. The rainbow can keep no promises; only the God of the rainbow can keep all promises. The God Who placed the mineral (ruby) in the earth is the only One Who can make us special and different for His glory!"

"With all of that in mind, keep your eye on the ruby!"

chapter twenty-seven

Thoughts I've Had About You and Me and Your Children

David Grafton

"*...and every winged fowl after his kind.*" (Genesis 1:21)

Check a tape of bird calls out of the library in order to learn which song belongs to which bird.

"*...he made the stars also.*" (Genesis 1:16)

Beg, borrow (but don't steal) a tent to pitch in the back yard to provide a place from which you and your child can study the stars.

The following ways to build a relationship with your family are not composed of completely new ideas. They do seem to be new though to so many who feel great watching some of these things on television or doing them in a restaurant or with an organization where activities are planned.

Don't let critics keep you from planning silly little events which are the stuff that make big show names and authors rich and most of all, are the times your family will remember.

Sometimes the child who scoffs at ten years of age will write up the unusual for the *Reader's Digest* in adulthood.

• Plant a fruit tree with your child leaving a permanent marker with names, date of planting, and kind of tree. *"...and the fruit tree yielding fruit after his kind..."* (Genesis 1:11)

• Find a private spot for you and your child to lie on your backs while you study the sky. *"...the greater light to rule the day..."* (Genesis 1:16)

• Look for an unattended apple or other fruit tree, find the owner, and ask to make a plan with him for unlimited picking of fruit by you and your children to distribute to the owner of the tree, neighbors, your own family, and the homeless. *"For none of us liveth to himself, and no man dieth to himself."* (Romans 14:7)

• As you ride in your car at night, point out the moon as it appears in different shapes and sizes from time to time. *"...the lesser light to rule the night..."* (Genesis 1:16)

• Go to garage sales to purchase extra toys, bikes, or sports equipment so there will be special things for your children's friends when they come to visit. *"Be kindly affectioned one to another with brotherly love; in honour preferring one another."* (Romans 12:10)

• Smile at your children. *"We then that are strong ought to bear the infirmities of the weak, and not to please ourselves."* (Romans 15:1)

• Look for an advertisement for an ant farm to study together. *"Go to the ant, thou sluggard; consider her ways, and be wise."* (Proverbs 6:6)

• Take time to go to the zoo when your child can linger as long as he wants at each stop. *"Let no man seek his own, but every man another's wealth."* (I Corinthians 10:24)

• Whether it be once a day, week, month or on special days, make a family ritual of raising and lowering the flag in your yard, giving thanks for and asking mercy for your country. *"If my people, which are called by my name, shall humble themselves, and pray, and seek my face, and turn from their wicked ways; then will I hear from heaven, and will forgive their sin, and will heal their land."* (II Chronicles 7:14)

• Pick up all kinds of outdoor clothes at garage sales or Goodwill for all kinds of weather so you can be ready for any activity and any friends who might be visiting. *"She is not afraid of the snow for her household: for all her household are clothed with scarlet."* (Proverbs 31:21)

• Have a box ready with picnic supplies—paper and plastic, salt and pepper, to be ready for the addition of bread, meat, and fruit from the grocery at any time. Put in a pair of binoculars with which to better enjoy nature. Let food served with a happy heart help provide a merry heart and therefore a continual feast. *"All the days of the afflicted are evil. but he that is of a merry heart hath a continual feast."* (Proverbs 15:15)

• Lead your children by your example to be examples to other adults. Encourage them to continue to live for the Lord, win souls, and keep high standards by doing those things yourselves. *"...Be thou an example of the believers, in word, in conversation, in charity, in spirit, in faith, in purity."* (I Timothy 4:12)

• Sit with a child while he experiments with a musical instrument. Pay attention to him and what he is doing. Make much of what some might think are little things. *"And it came to pass, when the evil spirit from God was upon Saul, that David took an harp, and played with his hand: so Saul was refreshed, and was well, and the evil spirit departed from him."* (I Samuel 16:23)

• Help your children work through their hurts and burdens without taking their burden from them. *"For every man shall bear his own burden."* (Galatians 6:5)

• When your child lets you know he wants to buy an item that you want him to have, set a future purchase date in order to enjoy anticipation, planning, and buying it together. *"Withhold not good from them to whom it is due, when it is in the power of thine hand to do it."* (Proverbs 3:27)

• Realize that if you make your home "children friendly," your house will not be so neat and pretty as you might like it. *"Where no oxen are, the crib is clean: but much increase is by the strength of the ox."* (Proverbs 14:4)

• Remember that a mother plotting with a child against his father will cause pain forever. *"And she put the skins of the kids of the goats upon his hands, and upon the smooth of his neck..."* (Genesis 27:16)

• Beg God to give you His vision for your children. *"Where there is no vision, the people perish: but he that keepeth the law, happy is he."* (Proverbs 29:18)

• Provide special clothing for your child which will identify the child as your child. *"And they sent the coat of many colours, and they brought it to their father; and said, This have we found: know now whether it be thy son's coat or no."* (Genesis 37:32)

• Work to never show favoritism to any of your children, thereby causing them to be jealous of a sibling. *"And when his brethren saw that their father loved him more than all his brethren, they hated him, and could not speak peaceably unto him."* (Genesis 37:4)

• Find something to make or do for a child who has to be away to help you keep focused on the child and therefore feeling close to him. *"Moreover his mother made him a little coat, and brought it to him from year to year, when she came up with her husband to offer the yearly sacrifice."* (I Samuel 2:19)

• Give your children to the Lord for as long as they live. *"Therefore also I have lent him to the LORD; as long as he liveth he shall be lent to the Lord. And he worshipped the LORD there."* (I Samuel 1:28)

• Lead your children to have a holy reverence of the Lord; to speak of Him, and to think of Him. There will be a book of remembrances for them. *"Then they that feared the LORD spake often one to another: and the LORD hearkened, and heard it, and a book of remembrance was written before him for them that feared the LORD, and that thought upon his name."* (Malachi 3:16)

• Be teachable. Children will learn more quickly from those they see learning. *"Thou therefore which teachest another, teachest thou not thyself? thou that preachest a man should not steal, dost thou steal?"* (Romans 2:21)

• Express thanks for every little thing that you receive and guide your children to do likewise. *"Giving thanks always for all things unto God and the Father in the name of our Lord Jesus Christ."* (Ephesians 5:20)

• Even if he has to choke out the words, help a child learn to say, "Will you forgive me?" *"...forgiving one another, even as God for Christ's sake hath forgiven you."* (Ephesians 4:32b)

• Spend time teaching your children respect for one another. Sibling rivalry is real just as lying and stealing is real. *"Let all bitterness, and wrath, and anger, and clamour, and evil speaking, be put away from you, with all malice."* (Ephesians 4:31)

• Work at submitting to all leadership. Children know who is the leader of the family before adults themselves do. We are always teaching whether it be negatively or positively. *"Wives, submit yourselves unto your own husbands, as unto the Lord."* (Ephesians 5:22)

• Help a child plan "others" into his budget no matter how small that budget might be. *"...that he may have to give to him that needeth."* (Ephesians 4:28c)

• Go with a child who has taken something that is not his in order to be by his side when he apologizes and returns what he has stolen. *"Let him that stole steal no more..."* (Ephesians 4:28a)

• Work by the side of a child until that child knows and enjoys work. *"...but rather let him labour, working with his hands the thing which is good..."* (Ephesians 4:28b)

• Help a child keep "short accounts" as you help him with daily even hourly attitude adjustments. *"Be ye angry, and sin not: let not the sun go down upon your wrath."* (Ephesians 4:26)

• "Hash" and "rehash" all the details should your child come home with something good, true, and positive, *"...but rejoiceth in the truth."* (I Corinthians 13:6b)

• Training your child to obey you is helping your child to do right. *"Children, obey your parents in the Lord: for this is right."* (Ephesians 6:1)

- Be quick to believe the good. *"...believeth all things."* (I Corinthians 13:7b)

- Go with a child to be a support to him while he apologizes for a lie told and proceeds to tell the truth. *"Wherefore putting away lying, speak every man truth with his neighbour: for we are members one of another."* (Ephesians 4:25)

- If your child should come home seemingly happy about someone getting into trouble, it is a good thing to pray a short prayer for the person in trouble. Ask your child if there is anything the two of you could do to help the person and then change the subject. *"...thinketh no evil."* (I Corinthians 13:5c)

- Encourage your child to plan what she's going to do for others on her birthday rather than to spend her time planning what others are going to do for her. *"...seeketh not her own."* (I Corinthians 13:5b)

- If your child's Sunday school teacher is new and inexperienced, motivate your child to be on the lookout for things he likes about the teacher and write encouraging notes about those things to his teacher. *"Beareth all things..."* (I Corinthians 13:7a)

- Take time to pray a simple little sentence with your child, thanking God for that about which he seems to be crediting only himself. *"...is not puffed up."* (I Corinthians 13:4e)

- When you are around a child who starts bragging on himself, try bragging on the child as fast as you can and perhaps he can leave the job for you to do. *"...charity vaunteth not itself."* (I Corinthians 13:4d)

• If possible give your child an attitude adjustment before he sees a friend with something you know he might want. *"...charity envieth not..."* (I Corinthians 13:4c)

• At every opportunity, answer a child's question concerning relationships with, "What would be the kind thing to do?" *"...and is kind."* (I Corinthians 13:4b)

• Allow children to see the realities of life. Let's not "protect" our children from the sicknesses, deaths and troubles of others that are such a part of our lives. *"Charity suffereth long..."* (I Corinthians 13:4a)

• Teach your child to hope for the best for and in others as long as others are alive. *"...hopeth all things."* (I Corinthians 13:7c)

• When your child comes home with a rumor, ask him questions that will help him see he has no proof of the gossip passed to him. *"...thinketh no evil."* (I Corinthians 13:5d)

• Use pleasant words to give health and sweetness of soul to your child. *"Pleasant words are as an honeycomb, sweet to the soul, and health to the bones."* (Proverbs 16:24)

• Use this verse as one test for your child's possible friendships. Ask yourself this question: "Will his soul be in danger should he learn the ways of a certain friend?" *"Make no friendship with an angry man; and with a furious man thou shalt not go: Lest thou learn his ways, and get a snare to thy soul."* (Proverbs 22:24, 25)

- Point out the end result of sin at every opportunity. *"Let not thine heart envy sinners: but be thou in the fear of the Lord all the day long."* (Proverbs 23:17)

- Practice speaking right things with your child. *"Yea, my reins shall rejoice, when thy lips speak right things."* (Proverbs 23:16)

- Be sure your children are properly supervised at all times. *"The rod and reproof give wisdom: but a child left to himself bringeth his mother to shame."* (Proverbs 29:15)

- Let's pray for wisdom to which children might attend. *"My son, attend unto my wisdom, and bow thine ear to my understanding."* (Proverbs 5:1)

- Take children to visit older people so they will be more able to follow this verse when they are adults. *"Hearken unto thy father that begat thee, and despise not thy mother when she is old."* (Proverbs 23:22)

- Be sure to wait for children to look you right in the eye when you are talking with them in order to promote hearing which, in turn, promotes wisdom. *"Hear thou, my son, and be wise, and guide thine heart in the way."* (Proverbs 23:19)

- Learn to control your eating habits so your children are not among gluttons when they are at home. *"Be not among winebibbers; among riotous eaters of flesh."* (Proverbs 23:20)

- Help children to begin thinking about the well being of the children they will someday rear. *"If thy children will keep my covenant and my testimony that I shall teach* them, their children shall also sit upon thy throne for evermore." (Psalms 132:12)

- For your own rest and delight, correct your child. *"Correct thy son, and he shall give thee rest; yea, he shall give delight unto thy soul."* (Proverbs 29:17)

- Live for the Lord for the sake of your children if for no other reason. *"Thou shalt not bow down thyself to them, nor serve them: for I the Lord thy God am a jealous God, visiting the iniquity of the fathers upon the children unto the third and fourth generation of them that hate me."* (Exodus 20:5)

- Teach children to be friendly to, but not friends with, unbelievers. *"Be ye not unequally yoked together with unbelievers: for what fellowship hath righteousness with unrighteousness? and what communion hath light with darkness?"* (II Corinthians 6:14)

- Be a just person for the sake of your children. *"The just man walketh in his integrity: his children are blessed after him."* (Proverbs 20:7)

- Work along with children to help them to learn to enjoy their work, avoiding slothfulness and wastefulness. *"He also that is slothful in his work is brother to him that is a great waster."* (Proverbs 18:9)

- Help children learn to know those rare times they should go to an authority to report someone else's misconduct. Do not encourage children to be tattletales. *"The words of a talebearer are as wounds, and they go down into the innermost parts of the belly."* (Proverbs 18:8)

• Show children how to call upon and praise the name of the Lord so they can be safe all their lives. *"The name of the L*ORD *is a strong tower: the righteous runneth into it, and is safe."* (Proverbs 18:10)

• Go for help to learn to show love, knowing that a child feeling well-loved will avoid a lot of foolishness. *"A foolish son is the calamity of his father: and the contentions of a wife are a continual dropping."* (Proverbs 19:13)

• Teach children to stay completely away from any teaching that does not line up with the Word of God. *"Cease, my son, to hear the instruction that causeth to err from the words of knowledge."* (Proverbs 19:27)

• Skip arm in arm with your child or teenager whenever your child feels comfortable allowing you to do so. *"...a time to embrace, and a time to refrain from embracing..."* (Ecclesiastes 3:5b)

• Be gracious, compassionate, merciful, and slow to anger which will cause us to "mother" children as the Lord "fathers" us. *"The L*ORD *is gracious, and full of compassion; slow to anger, and of great mercy."* (Psalms 145:8)

• Help a boy become a man by showing him how to put away childish things. *"When I was a child, I spake as a child, I understood as a child, I thought as a child: but when I became a man, I put away childish things."* (I Corinthians 13:11)

• Show children the importance of being good to all people. *"Be not forgetful to entertain strangers : for thereby some have entertained angels unawares."* (Hebrews 13:2)

• By your example, help your children learn to submit to authority. *"Obey them that have the rule over you, and submit yourselves: for they watch for your souls, as they that must give account, that they may do it with joy, and not with grief: for that is unprofitable for you."* (Hebrews 13:17)

• Help children learn to count every frustration as an opportunity to gain patience and, therefore, maturity. *"My brethren, count it all joy when ye fall into divers temptations; Knowing this, that the trying of your faith worketh patience."* (James 1:2, 3)

• Point out to children why your home is peaceful in the midst of a world of unrest. *"And the peace of God, which passeth all understanding, shall keep your hearts and minds through Christ Jesus."* (Philippians 4:7)

• Let church bus route children, Sunday school children, and your own children see you pray instead of fret. *"Be careful for nothing; but in every thing by prayer and supplication with thanksgiving let your requests be made known unto God."* (Philippians 4:6)

• Assign separate jobs for each child rather than, "Okay kids, you all pick up the toys." *"Let all things be done decently and in order."* (I Corinthians 14:40)

• If we want children to keep hope alive in their hearts, we must teach them how to live through their own tribulations and experiences. *"And not only so, but we glory in tribulations also: knowing that tribulation worketh patience; And patience, experience; and experience, hope."* (Romans 5:3, 4)

• Think on those things which stand the test of the eight characteristics in this verse in order to keep from becoming a gossip and from passing gossip or the gossip habit on to children. *"Finally, brethren, whatsoever things are true, whatsoever things are honest, whatsoever things are just, whatsoever things are pure, whatsoever things are lovely, whatsoever things are of good report; if there be any virtue, and if there be any praise, think on these things."* (Philippians 4:8)

chapter twenty-eight

*K*ids Without Chaos

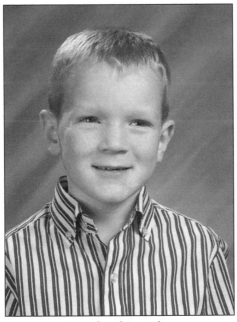

Michael Sparks

"And God set them in the firmament of the heaven to give light upon the earth." (Genesis 1:17)

Look for a good used telescope to use with your children to help them learn to enjoy God's creation.

When the title of this book was mentioned to our good friend, Dr. Tom Vogel, he asked, "Oh, is Mrs. Evans writing fiction again?" I had a good laugh about that statement because to some, having kids without constant chaos does seem like fiction. The best way to live out the title of this book is to begin by knowing for sure you are on your way to Heaven. Are you 100 percent sure if you were to die today you would go to Heaven? You can know!

In I John 5:13, the Bible says, *"These things have I written unto you that believe on the name of the Son of God; that ye may know that ye have eternal life."* You can **know** you are on your way to Heaven.

1. You Are a Sinner.

In Romans 3:10, the Bible says, *"As it is written, There is none righteous, no, not one,"* and in verse 23, *"For all have sinned, and come short of the glory of God."* These verses mean that everyone sins, and that means you are a sinner also.

2. As a Sinner, You Owe a Sin Debt

In Romans 5:12a, the Bible tells us from where sin came: *"Wherefore, as by one man sin entered into the world, and death by sin; and so death passed upon all men, for that all have sinned."* This means Adam committed the first sin in the whole world. This word, "death," doesn't mean just dying and going to the grave; it means eternal separation from God in a lake of fire. This is our punishment for our sin, and a debt you owe as of right now.

But, thankfully, the story doesn't end there! In Romans 6:23, the Bible says, *"For the wages of sin is death; but the gift of God is eternal life through Jesus Christ our Lord."* Going to Heaven is a gift; it's absolutely free!

3. Your Good Works Will Not Pay Your Sin Debt or Get You to Heaven.

"For by grace are ye saved through faith; and that not of yourselves: it is the gift of God: Not of works, lest any man should boast." (Ephesians 2:8, 9)

4. Jesus Has Already Paid Your Sin Debt.

"But God commendeth his love toward us, in that, while we were yet sinners, Christ died for us." (Romans 5:8)

5. Accept His Gift Today.

If you know that you're a sinner, you realize there is a penalty for that sin, and that you can't pay for it yourself, and you realize that Jesus died on the cross and shed His blood for your sins, this is what you need to do. In Romans 10:9 and 13, the Bible says, *"That if thou shalt confess with thy mouth the Lord Jesus, and shalt believe in thine heart that God hath raised him from the dead, thou shalt be saved. For whosoever shall call upon the name of the Lord shall be saved."* "Whosoever" means you. We could put your name in the blanks: "For ___ shall call upon the name of the Lord and ___ shall be saved."

If you will trust Jesus to take you to Heaven when you die, pray this prayer: "Dear Jesus, forgive me of my sins. I trust You today, Jesus, and only You to take me to Heaven when I die. Thank You for saving me. Amen."

According to the Bible, if you were to die today, you would go to Heaven because in John 3:36 the Bible says, *"He that believeth on the Son hath everlasting life."*

If you have trusted Jesus as your Saviour, please write or call us so that we may rejoice with you. May God bless you as you begin your new life in Christ.

Christian Womanhood
8400 Burr Street
Crown Point, Indiana 46307
219-365-3202

The pictures used throughout this book are in no way affiliated with any material or particular chapter. For example, everyone who knows Alexander Carver on page 77 thinks he is a gifted child, but that picture was not placed there with the chapter title in mind. The pictures simply represent the many children Mrs. Evans knows and enjoys as friends.

———

Any materials mentioned in this book as suggested reading are available through:
Christian Womanhood
8400 Burr Street
Crown Point, Indiana 46307
219-365-3202